שָׁלוֹם וּבְרָכָה

The New Hebrew Primer

Pearl Tarnor • Carol Levy

לשמואל יחזקאל

מסבתא

לקובי ורעה

מאמא

ושננתם לבניך

"And you shall teach them diligently to your children."

Activities by Roberta Osser Baum, Rae Eskin, and Aviva Lucas Gutnick

Editorial consultants: Ellen Rank, Terry Kaye

Special thanks to Danielle Greene for creating the Hebrew files for the revised edition
and to Judy Sandman for proofreading the revised edition.

Artwork by: Joni Levy Liberman (chapter openers); Deborah Zemke (activity art)

Published by Behrman House, Inc.
Millburn, New Jersey 07041
www.behrmanhouse.com

ISBN 978-1-68115-161-8

Library of Congress Control Number: 2023951773

Design by Zatar Creative
Revised edition project manager: Aviva Lucas Gutnick
Original edition project manager: Terry Kaye

Printed in China

1 3 5 7 9 8 6 4 2

TABLE OF CONTENTS

LESSON 1

שַׁבָּת

Shabbat

NEW LETTERS

בּ ת תּ שׁ

NEW VOWELS

ַ ָ

BET

1 בַּ בַּ בַּ בַּ בַּ בַּ

2 בָּ בָּ בָּ בָּ בָּ בָּ

3 בּ בַּ בּ בָּ בַּ בּ

4 בַּבַּ בַּבָּ בּבָּ בּבַּ בַּבָּ בָּבַּ

SHAPE IT UP

What does ***Bet*** look like?
Close your eyes and picture the letter.
Draw it in the air or use your whole body to make the shape of the letter ***Bet***.

Make up a clue to remember ***Bet***.

What do ַ and ָ sound like?

Make a hand motion to show the shape of ַ and ָ as you say their sound.

I SPY

Read aloud each line.

Find the sound that's different from the others.

Circle it or highlight it.

1. בּ בּ בּ בַּ בּ בּ
2. בָּ בָּ בּ בָּ בָּ בָּ
3. בּ בַּ בּ בּ בּ בּ
4. בַּ בַּ בַּ בּ בַּ בַּ

SOUNDS LIKE

Clap your hands as you read aloud each line. Which two Hebrew sounds are the same? Circle them or tell a partner.

1. בַּ בּ בָּ
2. בּ בַּ בּ
3. בּ בָּ בָּ
4. בָּ בָּ בּ
5. בּ בַּ בּ
6. בָּ בּ בַּ

1. תַ תָּ תַּ תָ תַּ תַּ
2. תָּ תָ תּ תָּ תַ ת

TAV

SHAPE IT UP

What does ***Tav*** look like? Close your eyes and picture the letter. Draw it in the air or use your whole body to make the shape of the letter ***Tav***.

Make up a clue to remember ***Tav***.

HEADS UP!

The letters ת and תּ make the same sound.

Say that sound aloud.

READY, SET, READ

Read each line below softly. Read the lines again loudly.

תַּ בַּ בּ תָּ תַּ תַּ 1

בָּ בּ תּ תָּ תַ בַּ 2

תַּת תָּתָּ תָּת תַּבָּ תַּבַּ תַּת 3

תַּבָּ תַּבּ בַּת תַּבַּ בַּת תַבּ 4

בַּת בָּתָּ תָּבּ בָּבּ תַּבּ בַּת 5

תַּבָּת בַּתָּת תַּבָּבּ בָּבָּת בַּבַּת 6

Great job!

EXTRA CREDIT

How many times did you read the Hebrew word for ***daughter***?

______

I KNOW HEBREW!

Can you find this Hebrew word above?

daughter = בַּת

Read and circle or highlight it.

WORD RIDDLE

I am written on a scroll. I am kept in the Ark. I am read in the synagogue.

My name begins with the letter תּ.

What am I?

I SPY

Read aloud each line.

Find the sound that's different from the others. Jump up and say the name of that letter..

בּ	בּ	תּ	בּ	בּ	בּ	1
תּ	תּ	תּ	תּ	בּ	תּ	2
תּ	בּ	בּ	בּ	בּ	בּ	3
ת	ת	ת	בּ	ת	ת	4
תּ	תּ	תּ	תּ	תּ	בּ	5
בּ	תּ	בּ	בּ	בּ	בּ	6

SHIN

ש

שַׁ	שָׁ	שׁ	שַׁ	שָׁ	שָׁ	1
שַׁ	שָׁ	שָׁ	שַׁ	שׁ	שַׁ	2

שַׁשָׁ	שָׁשָׁ	שָׁשַׁ	שָׁשׁ	3

SHAPE IT UP

What does ***Shin*** look like?

Close your eyes and picture the letter. Draw it in the air or use your whole body to make the shape of the letter ***Shin***.

Make up a clue to remember ***Shin***.

READY, SET, READ

Read the lines below as fast as you can. Try to read them again even faster!

1 בָּ בַּ בּ בַּ בָּ בּ

2 תָּ תַ תּ תָּ תַ ת

3 שַׁשׁ שַׁב שָׁת שָׁשַׁ שָׁבַ שָׁתָּ

4 בַּשׁ תָּשׁ בַּת שַׁתַּ בָּשָׁ בַּת

5 שַׁבַּשׁ תָּשַׁב תַּבָּשׁ תַּבַּת בַּשָׁת

6 שַׁבַּב בַּתָּב תָּתַּב בַּבָּת תַּבַּת

7 תַּבָּת שַׁבַּתָּ בַּשָׁת בַּשָׁשׁ בַּבָּת

8 שַׁבָּת שַׁבָּת שַׁבָּת שַׁבָּת שַׁבָּת

I KNOW HEBREW!

Can you find this Hebrew word above?

Shabbat = שַׁבָּת

Read and circle or highlight it.

EXTRA CREDIT

God created the world in six days. On the seventh day God rested.

Which line contains the name of that special day?

_____

I SPY

Read aloud each line.

Find the Hebrew that sounds the same as the English in the box.

Circle it or sing it out loud.

שַׁ	בּ	ת	תַּ	בַּ	שׁ	BAH	1
בּ	תּ	תָּ	שָׁ	שׁ	בָּ	TAH	2
בּ	שָׁ	בָּ	תַּ	שׁ	בַּ	B	3
בַּ	בּ	תַּ	שָׁ	שׁ	תּ	SHAH	4
שׁ	בָּ	תָּ	שׁ	תַ	ת	T	5
שַׁ	שׁ	בּ	תּ	תָּ	שָׁ	SH	6

CONNECTIONS

Connect each Hebrew letter to its name.

What sound does each letter make?

HEADS UP!

Bet (בּ) makes the sound ______.

Tav (תּ or ת) makes the sound ______.

Shin (שׁ) makes the sound ______.

What do you notice about the names of these Hebrew letters and the sounds the letters make?

WRITING PRACTICE

בּ

תּ ת

שׁ

Write the Hebrew word for ***daughter***.

בַּת

Write the Hebrew word for ***Shabbat***.

שַׁבָּת

MAKE A MATCH

What is the name of each letter?

Write the letter on the line.

1	תּ	BET	TAV	SHIN	תּ
2	בּ	TAV	SHIN	BET	
3	שׁ	SHIN	BET	TAV	
4	ת	TAV	BET	SHIN	

OUR TRADITION – שַׁבָּת

שַׁבָּת means "rest."
God created the world in six days.
On the seventh day, God rested.
We call that special day שַׁבָּת.

How do you rest and relax?
Draw a picture of yourself doing that.

WELCOMING שַׁבָּת

On Friday evening when Shabbat begins, we welcome it with blessings and songs.

Write the word שַׁבָּת on the line below each object we use to welcome שַׁבָּת.

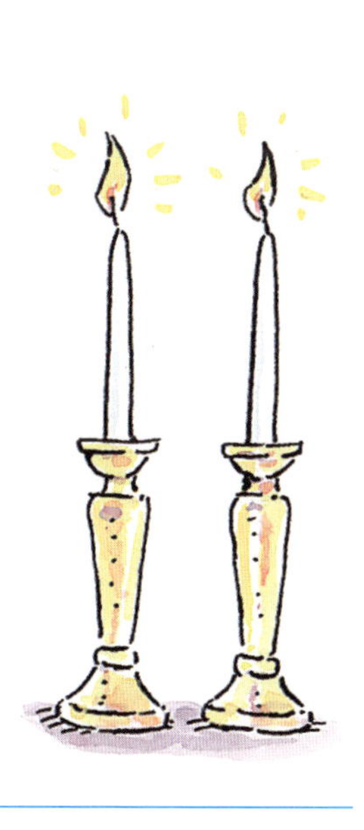

Helper

NEW LETTER

LETTERS YOU KNOW. Say the name and sound of each letter.

בּ ת תּ שׁ

VOWELS YOU KNOW. Say the sound of each vowel.

◌ַ ◌ָ

1 מַ מָ מ מָ מ מַ

2 מַ בּ ת תָּ מָ שָׁ

3 מַ מָ שׁ שַׁ מָ שׁ

SHAPE IT UP

What does ***Mem*** look like?

Close your eyes and picture the letter.

Draw it in the air or use your whole body to make the shape of the letter ***Mem***.

Make up a clue to remember ***Mem***.

READY, SET, READ

Read the first two lines s-l-o-w-l-y. Read them again correctly as fast as you can.
Take turns with a partner reading every other line at a regular pace.

1 שַׁמָ מָשׁ מַמָ מָשׁ שַׁבָּ בָּת

2 מַשׁ מַבּ מָת מַמַ מַתַּ מַבָּ

3 בַּמַ שָׁמָ תָּמָ בַּת בָּמָ תַמַ

4 מָשַׁבּ מַתָּשׁ מַבַּת מַמַת בָּמָשׁ

5 תָּמַשׁ שַׁבָּת תַּמַת מַבָּשׁ מָשַׁשׁ

6 שַׁבָּת שַׁמָשׁ מָתָּשׁ מָשַׁשׁ שַׁמָשׁ

7 שַׁמָ שַׁמָשׁ שַׁבָּ שַׁבָּת שַׁמָשׁ

8 שַׁבָּת שַׁמָשׁ שַׁבָּת שַׁמָשׁ שַׁבָּת

I KNOW HEBREW!

Can you find this Hebrew word above?
helper candle on the* hanukkiyah*,
the Hanukkah menorah = שַׁמָשׁ
Read it, then circle or point to it each time you find it.

EXTRA CREDIT

How many times did you read the word for ***helper***?

______

I SPY

Find the English that sounds the same as the Hebrew in the box.

Circle it or sing it out loud.

T	M	B	SH	ת	1
MAH	SHAH	SH	TAH	שַׁ	2
M	TAH	MAH	BAH	מָ	3
MAH	SH	TAH	SHAH	שׁ	4
BAH	T	B	TAH	בָּ	5

WORD RIDDLE

You eat me on Passover. I am flat and crunchy. My name begins with the letter מ. What am I?

Draw a picture of me with your favorite topping or tell a partner about your favorite topping for me.

WRITING PRACTICE

מ

Write the Hebrew word for ***helper***.

שַׁמָּשׁ

Write the Hebrew word for ***Shabbat***.

שַׁבָּת

How did you do? Circle your best ***Mem*** above.

OUR TRADITION — שַׁמָּשׁ

שַׁמָּשׁ means "helper." The שַׁמָּשׁ is the helper candle on the ***hanukkiyah***, the Hanukkah menorah.

We use the שַׁמָּשׁ to light the other candles.

What do you think is special about using a שַׁמָּשׁ to light a Hanukkah menorah?

CONNECTIONS

Say the sound of each letter.

Match each letter to the picture whose name begins with the same sound.

ת

NAME THAT LETTER

Write the Hebrew letter under its name.

SHIN	BET	TAV	MEM
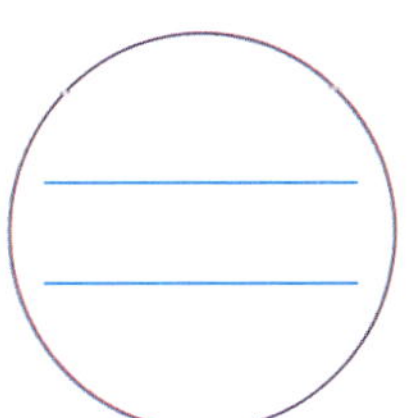	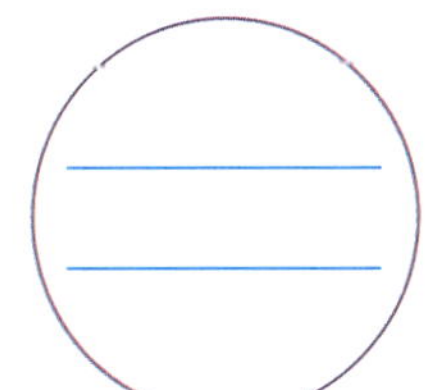	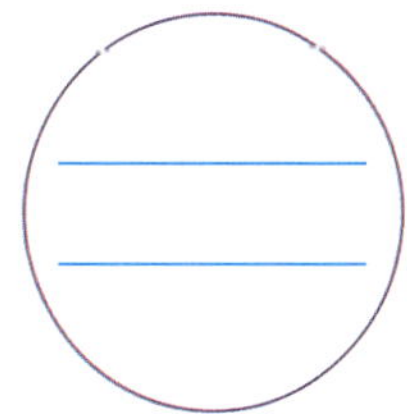	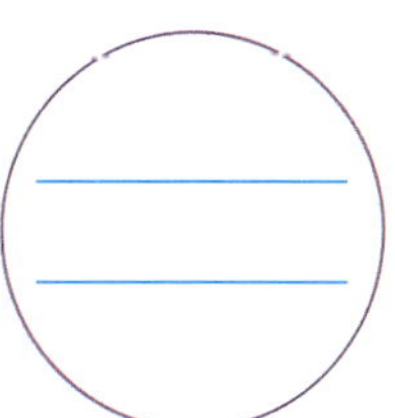

LESSON 3

כַּלָה

Bride

NEW LETTERS

ל כּ ה

LETTERS YOU KNOW. Say the name and sound of each letter.

בּ ת תּ שׁ מ

VOWELS YOU KNOW. Say the sound of each vowel.

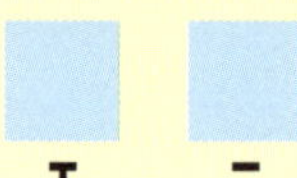

LAMED

ל

1	לַ	לָ	ל	לָ	ל	לַ
2	לָ	לַ	ל	מַ	מָ	מ
3	לָ	בָּ	תַּ	שַׁ	מָ	תָ

SHAPE IT UP

What does ***Lamed*** look like? Close your eyes and picture the letter. Draw it in the air or use your whole body to make the shape of the letter ***Lamed***.

Make up a clue to remember ***Lamed***.

READY, SET, READ

Read the odd-numbered lines to a partner. Have a partner read the even-numbered lines to you.

1	שׁ	שַׁ	בַּ	בּ	תַּ	תָ
2	תַּל	שַׁל	לָתּ	לָשׁ	מַמָ	לַמָ
3	לַבַּ	לָל	לַתַּ	לָשָׁ	לָמָ	לַתּ
4	מַל	תַּל	שָׁל	בַּל	לַל	שָׁמָ
5	מַמָשׁ	מַלָת	בָּלַת	שָׁלַשׁ	בַּת	
6	מָלַל	לַבַּת	תָּלַל	מָשָׁל	מָלַל	
7	בַּלָשׁ	שַׁמָשׁ	תָּלַשׁ	שָׁלָל	לַמָשׁ	
8	שַׁמָשׁ	לַשַׁמָשׁ	שַׁבָּת	לַשַׁבָּת	שַׁמָשׁ	

BONUS

Choose any word for a partner to read. Then have a partner choose any word for you to read. Continue until you've each read four words. Challenge each other with the long words!

EXTRA CREDIT

How many times did you read the word for ***helper***? ______

How many times did you read the word for ***daughter***? ______

SOUNDS LIKE

Read aloud each word on line 1.

Circle the Hebrew sounds that are the same.

Show a partner and have your partner read them.

Repeat for the other lines.

מָשׁ	מָשָׁ	שַׁמַ	מַשׁ	1
שַׁל	שַׁלַ	שָׁלָ	לָשָׁ	2
תַּבּ	בָּת	בַּת	בַּתָ	3
לָבַּ	לַבּ	בַּלָ	לַבָּ	4
מַל	לָמָ	לַמַ	לַל	5

I SPY

Read aloud each line.

Find and circle the Hebrew that sounds the same as the English in the box.

בַּ	לַ	שׁ	תַּ	ל	LAH	1
ל	בּ	ת	מ	מָ	M	2
מ	תַּ	מַ	בַּ	שַׁ	MAH	3
תּ	לַ	בּ	שׁ	ל	L	4
מַ	בּ	שׁ	בַּ	שַׁ	SHAH	5

KAF

כּ	כַּ	כָּ	כּ	כָּ	כַּ	1
מַ	שַׁ	ת	ל	בָּ	כַּ	2
מַ	כַּ	בָּ	ת	כַּ	בָּ	3

READY, SET, READ

Read each line as s-l-o-w-l-y as you can. Read again only the sounds or words that have a ***Lamed***. Then read only the sounds or words that start with a ***Kaf***.

1 כַּ כָּ כּ בָּ בַּ בּ

2 כַּבָּ כַּלָ כָּמָ כָּשׁ כַּת כָּשָׁ

3 לַכָּ מַכָּ תַּכַּ בַּכָּ שָׁכַּ כָּלָ

4 לָמָ בַּלָ תַּכַּ שָׁמָ מָכָּ בַּת

5 כַּבַּת מַכַּת כַּלָשׁ כָּלַל תַּכַּת

6 כַּלַת כָּלַל כָּתַשׁ כָּשַׁל בָּלָת

7 שַׁמָשׁ שַׁמָשׁ שַׁבָּת שַׁבָּת מַמָשׁ

8 שַׁבָּת לַשַׁבָּת שַׁבָּת כַּשַׁבָּת כַּשַׁבָּת

SHAPE IT UP

What does ***Kaf*** look like? Close your eyes and picture the letter.
Draw it in the air or use your whole body to make the shape of the letter ***Kaf***.

Make up a clue to remember ***Kaf***.

LETTER BOXES

Say the name of the letter in each box. Circle or point to the sound each letter makes. Say the sound.

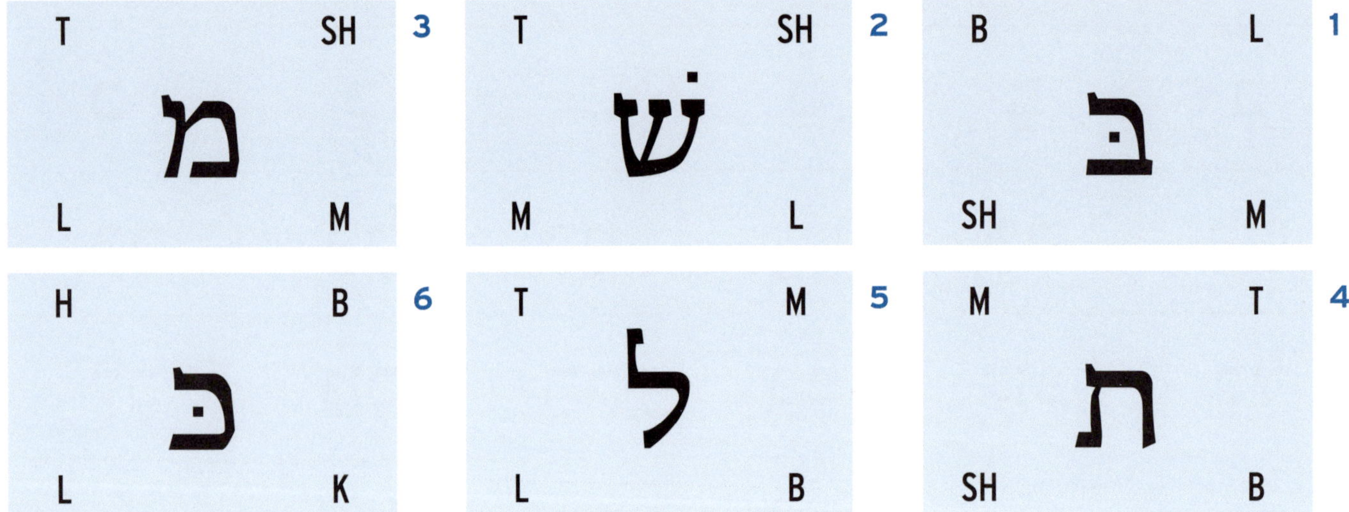

HAY

ה

הַ הָ ה הַ ה הָ 1

הַ כַּ לָ מָ שַׁ הָ 2

הַ מָ הַ הָ שָׁ הָ 3

SHAPE IT UP

What does ***Hay*** look like?
Close your eyes and picture the letter.
Draw it in the air or use your whole body to make the shape of the letter ***Hay***.

Make up a clue to remember ***Hay***.

HEADS UP!

The letter ה is pronounced "h," but when ה comes at the end of the word and has no vowel under it, it is silent.

READY, SET, READ

Find and read all the sounds and words that start with a ***Hay***. Then read all the sounds and words that end with a ***Hay***. Find and read all the sounds and words that do not have a ***Hay***.

Which sound made you laugh? (Hint: it's on line 2.)

בַּ הָ תָּ הַ כַּ הָ 1

הַל הָבּ הַתּ הָשׁ הָת הַהָ 2

בָּה תָּה שַׁה לָה מַה הַה 3

תָּלָה בָּמָה לָשָׁה כַּמָה שַׁבָּת 4

לָמָה מַכָּה שָׁמָב כַּלָב לָשָׁה 5

הַבַּת הַשַׁמָשׁ הַשַׁבָּת הַמָשָׁל הַכַּלָה 6

כַּלָה הַכַּלָה מַכָּה כַּמָה לָמָה לָשָׁה 7

שַׁבָּת הַכַּלָה שַׁבָּת הַכַּלָה שַׁבָּת הַכַּלָה 8

I KNOW HEBREW!

Can you find these Hebrew words above?

the Sabbath bride = שַׁבָּת הַכַּלָה

bride = כַּלָה

Read and circle or highlight them.

EXTRA CREDIT

How many times did you read the words for ***Sabbath bride***?

_____

WRITING PRACTICE

ל

כּ

ה

Write the Hebrew word for ***bride***.

כַּלָּה

Write the Hebrew words for the ***Sabbath bride***.

שַׁבָּת הַכַּלָּה

How did you do?

I SPY

Read each line.

Circle or highlight the English that sounds the same as the Hebrew letter in the box.

Write the Hebrew letter on the line or tell a partner the name of the letter.

1	שׁ	T	SH	H	V	
2	כּ	B	M	K	SH	
3	ל	S	H	G	L	
4	ה	H	T	SH	M	
5	בּ	SH	K	S	B	
6	ת	L	T	S	H	
7	מ	T	H	M	SH	

OUR TRADITION — כַּלָּה

Every Friday evening as we welcome שַׁבָּת, we say that שַׁבָּת is like a bride, כַּלָּה.

Just as a כַּלָּה is joyously welcomed at the wedding ceremony,
so we welcome שַׁבָּת with great happiness.

What are some ways that שַׁבָּת is like a כַּלָּה?

WORD MATCH

Match each Hebrew term with its English meaning. Read each Hebrew-English match aloud.

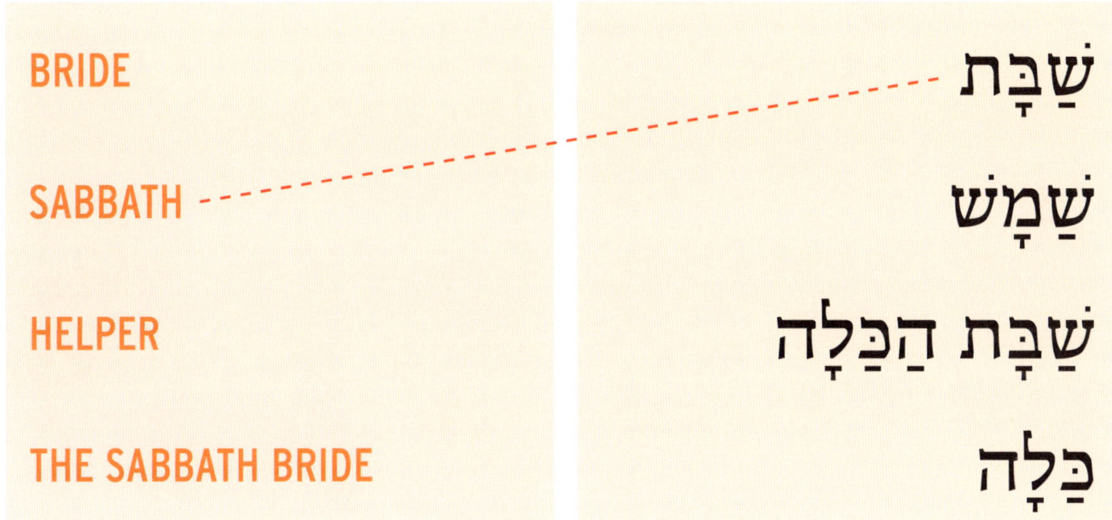

ALEF BET CHART

You know these Hebrew letters:

בּ תּ ת שׁ מ ל כּ ה

Turn to the ***Alef Bet*** chart on page 160. Color in the letters you have learned.

You will return to the chart again after a few more lessons.

The more letters you learn, the more colorful the ***Alef Bet*** chart will become.

LESSON 4

בְּרָכָה

Blessing

NEW LETTERS

ר כ

NEW VOWEL

ְ

LETTERS YOU KNOW. Say the name and sound of each letter.

בּ ת תּ שׁ מ ל כּ ה

VOWELS YOU KNOW. Say the sound of each vowel.

ָ ַ

RESH

ר

ְ

1	רַ	רָ	רְ	רְ	רַ	ר
2	בְּ	תְּ	שְׁ	מְ	לְ	כְּ
3	רַ	רְ	בְּ	בַּ	שָׁ	שְׁ

SHAPE IT UP

What does ***Resh*** look like?
Close your eyes and picture the letter.
Draw it in the air or use your whole body to make the shape of the letter ***Resh***
Make up a clue to remember ***Resh***.

What does ְ sound like?

Make a hand motion to show the shape of ְ as you say its sound.

READY, SET, READ

Read aloud the lines below. Then read all the words with the ְ vowel. Remember, that vowel is often, but not always, silent. It makes a very short sound when it appears under the first letter in a word.

1 רַ ר מַ מְ לְ ל

2 שָׁר כַּר שָׁרָ כָּרָ רַבּ רַבָּ

3 רַבּ רַת רַשׁ רַל רָה רָמָ

4 בַּר תַּר מַר שָׁר כַּר הַר

5 רַבָּה כָּרָה תָּשַׁר רָמָה רָשַׁל

6 הָרָה מָרָה שָׁרָה רַכָּה שָׁמַר

7 רָשַׁל לְבַּר שַׁמָשׁ שָׁמַר שָׁרַת הַכָּרָה

8 שָׁמְרָה מַלְכָּה רָשְׁמָה הַכָּרָה שַׁבָּת הַמַלְכָּה

I KNOW HEBREW!

Can you find this Hebrew word above?
What line is it on?

queen = מַלְכָּה

Read the word the way you think a queen would read it. Don't forget to put on your (pretend) crown!

EXTRA CREDIT

Can you find the word for ***helper***?

Write it here. ____________

NAME TAG

Match the Hebrew with its name on each line. Say the sound of each letter.

HAY	TAV	SHIN	תּ	1
SHIN	KAF	BET	בּ	2
RESH	HAY	TAV	ר	3
HAY	SHIN	BET	שׁ	4
KAF	HAY	TAV	ה	5
MEM	SHIN	LAMED	ל	6
LAMED	KAF	BET	כּ	7
MEM	LAMED	TAV	מ	8

CHAF

כ

1 כַ כָ כְ כ כָ כְ

2 כַּ כָ כְּ כְ כָּ כָ

3 כְ כְּ בָּ כָּ כַ בַּ

HEADS UP!

The letters כ and כּ make different sounds.

What sound does כ make?
What sound does כּ make?

Practice making those two sounds.

SHAPE IT UP

What does **Chaf** look like?
Close your eyes and picture the letter.

Draw it in the air or use your whole body to make the shape of the letter **Chaf**.

Make up a clue to help you remember the difference between **Kaf** and **Chaf**.

READY, SET, READ

Read lines 1-4 in a happy 🙂 voice. Read lines 5-8 in a sad 🙁 voice.

1 מָכַ בָּכָ כָּכָ רָכַ תָּכָ לְכָ

2 כָּה מָכַ כָּכָ כַבָּ כַּת כַשְׁ

3 רַכְ כָּמְ שַׁכְ כַּר תַּכַ בַּר

4 בָּכָה כָּכָה רַכָּה מָכַר שָׁכַר כַּלַת

5 כַּלָה כָּהָה כַּמָה מַכָּה רָכַשׁ לַכַּת

6 בָּכַת כָּכַת כָּרָה לְכָה תָּכָה לָכַשׁ

7 בָּכְתָה הַתָּכָה כָּרַכְתָּ מָכְרָה הָלַכְתָּ

8 הָלַכְתְּ בְּרָכָה בְּרָכָה הָלְכָה מָשְׁכָה

I KNOW HEBREW!

Can you find this Hebrew word above?

blessing = בְּרָכָה

How many times did you read the word for ***blessing***?

______

EXTRA CREDIT

Can you find a word above that sounds like another English word for automobile? (Hint: it's on line 3).

What Hebrew letters are in that word?

RHYME TIME

Read the Hebrew words in each column When you find two that rhyme, connect them and sing those words out loud.

1	בָּכָה	כַּר
2	הַר	מָרָה
3	מַכָּה	כָּכָה
4	כַּמָּה	מָשָׁל
5	שָׂרָה	רַכָּה
6	שָׁלָל	לָמָה

I SPY

Read aloud each line.

Find the sound that's different from the others. Circle or highlight it. Then, say the name of that letter.

1 בּ בּ בּ תּ בּ בּ בּ

2 כּ כּ כּ כּ כּ בּ כּ

3 ת ת ת ת ת ת ה

4 כ ת כ כ כ כ כ

5 ה ה ר ה ה ה ה

6 כ כ כ כּ כ כ כ

WRITING PRACTICE

ר

כ

Write the Hebrew word for ***blessing***.

בְּרָכָה

Write the Hebrew word for ***queen***.

מַלְכָּה

How did you do? Circle your best ***Chaf*** and your best ***Resh*** above.

ODD ONE OUT

Find the letter on each line that doesn't belong. Write it on the line.

1	תּ	תּ	תּ	תּ	בּ	תּ	______
2	ה	ה	ה	ר	ה	ה	______
3	שׁ	ל	שׁ	שׁ	שׁ	שׁ	______
4	ת	ת	כ	ת	ת	ת	______
5	תּ	תּ	תּ	כּ	תּ	תּ	______
6	בּ	בּ	בּ	בּ	מ	בּ	______

OUR TRADITION – בְּרָכָה

A בְּרָכָה is a blessing.

When we say a בְּרָכָה we praise God for the gifts God gives us.

For example, we praise God for the food we eat, for the Shabbat wine we drink, and even for a rainbow that stretches across the sky.

What do you praise or thank God for? Write it or draw it here.

WORDS YOU KNOW

Read each of the words below to a partner. Have your partner say the meaning of the word. Then switch. Do you know the meanings of all the words?

שַׁבָּת　שַׁמָּשׁ　כַּלָּה　בְּרָכָה　מַלְכָּה

EXTRA CREDIT

Can you use each Hebrew word in an English sentence?

Example: We welcome שַׁבָּת by lighting candles.

LESSON 5

הַבְדָּלָה

Havdalah
Separation

NEW LETTERS

ב ד

NEW VOWEL

◌ֲ

LETTERS YOU KNOW. Say the name and sound of each letter.

בּ ת תּ שׁ מ ל כּ ה ר כ

VOWELS YOU KNOW. Say the sound of each vowel.

◌ַ ◌ָ ◌ְ

VET

ב

◌ֲ

1	בַ	בָ	בְ	בָ	בַ	בְ
2	הֲ	הַ	בַ	בַּ	בְ	בְּ
3	כַ	בַ	כְ	בְ	כ	ב

SHAPE IT UP

What does ***Vet*** look like?
Close your eyes and picture the letter.
Draw it in the air or use your whole body to make the shape of the letter ***Vet***.

Make up a clue to help you remember the difference between ***Vet*** and ***Bet***.

What does ◌ֲ sound like?

Make a hand motion to show the shape of ◌ֲ as you say its sound.

READY, SET, READ

Read all the words that contain a ***Bet***. Then read all the words that contain a ***Vet***.
Find and read all the words that don't contain a ***Bet*** or a ***Vet***.

1	בָּב	כָּב	תָּב	רָב	הָב	שָׁב
2	תָּבָּ	שָׁב	מַבָּ	הַב	כָּבַ	בַּת
3	לַב	רַב	כָּב	בַּל	מַב	הָבָ
4	שָׁרַב	שָׁבָה	כָּתַב	לָבַשׁ	הָבָה	
5	לַבָּה	בָּבָה	רַבָּה	שָׁבַר	רָבָה	
6	לַבְלָר	רְבָבָה	שָׁבַרְתָּ	כָּתַבְתָּ	הֲבָרָה	
7	לְהָבָה	הֲרָמָה	הֲלָכָה	הֲמָרָה	כָּתְבָה	
8	הֲשָׁבָה	הֲתַשָׁה	הַתָּרָה	מְבַלָּה	הֲלְכָה	

EXTRA CREDIT

Find the words that contain both a ***Bet*** and a ***Vet***.

How many words did you find? ____

HEADS UP!

The vowels ָ, ֲ, ַ make the same sound.

Say that sound.

WORD WIZARD

A word you've learned is hidden below.
Cross out the Hebrew letters and vowels that match the English sounds below.
Write the remaining Hebrew letters and their vowels on the lines below to discover the hidden word.

1	SHAH	4	HAH
2	V	5	K
3	LAH	6	T

שַׁ בְּ בְ לָ רָ הָ כָ כְּ ה ת

______ ______ ______ ______

______ ______ ______ ______

What does the word mean? ________

DALET

ד

1 דַ דָ דְ דַ דְ ד

2 הֲ רַ דְ רְ כָ דָ

3 דַ רַ דָ רָ ד ר

SHAPE IT UP

What does ***Dalet*** look like? Close your eyes and picture the letter.
Draw it in the air or use your whole body to make the shape of the letter ***Dalet***.

Make up a clue to remember ***Dalet***.

READY, SET, READ

Read aloud the odd-numbered lines below in a funny voice.
Read the even-numbered lines in your regular voice.

1 דָד דָר בַּד בַּר דָשׁ רָשׁ

2 דָשׁ דַת דַל דָה דָר דָב

3 מַד כַּד בַּדָ שַׁדָ הַד רַד

4 דָלָה דָבָר דְבַשׁ לָמַד הָדָר דָרָה

5 מָדַד דָשָׁה שָׁדַד דָרַשׁ דָהָה לְבַד

6 הֲמָרָה דְמָמָה הֲלָכָה הֲדָרָה הֲבָרָה

7 כָּתְבָה לָבַשְׁתְּ לָמְדָה דָרַכְתָּ מָדְדָה

8 הַבְדָלָה דְרָשָׁה הֲלָכָה בְּרָכָה הַבְדָלָה

I KNOW HEBREW!

Can you find this Hebrew word above?

havdalah, separation = הַבְדָלָה

Read it and circle or highlight it.

EXTRA CREDIT

How many times did you read the word for ***separation***?

____

SOUNDS LIKE

Read the Hebrew in each box.

Then read the Hebrew on each line. When you hear a sound the same as the sound in the box, snap your fingers.

הָרָ	הַבַ	תַבַ	הָבָ	1
כַּד	בַּרְ	בָּדְ	בַּד	2
רָשַׁ	רָתָה	דָשָׁה	רָשָׁה	3
כַּבְ	בָּבְ	כַּכְ	כָּכְ	4
דַבַר	רָבָד	דָבַה	דָבָר	5

I SPY

Find and read the Hebrew that sounds the same as the English in the box. Circle it or tell a partner.

הַ	תַ	רָ	רְ	בְ	דַ	RAH	1
הֲ	ה	כַּ	בּ	כְ	כְּ	KAH	2
בְ	בּ	תְ	ר	בַ	כַ	V	3
דַ	כְ	רְ	דְ	רַ	ה	D	4
רַ	הֲ	דַ	ה	מַ	תַ	HAH	5
כְ	רְ	כַּ	בְּ	שׁ	כְּ	K	6

WRITING PRACTICE

ב בּ ב

ד ד ד

Write the Hebrew word for ***havdalah, separation***.

הַבְדָּלָה הַבְדָּלָה הַבְדָּלָה

Write the Hebrew word for ***Shabbat***.

שַׁבָּת שַׁבָּת שַׁבָּת

How did you do? Circle your best ***Vet*** and your best ***Dalet*** above.

NAME TAG

Read aloud the name of the Hebrew letter in each box. Find its matching Hebrew letter and write it on the line.

1	LAMED	מ	ל	ד	ה	ל
2	HAY	ר	ב	ה	ת	
3	VET	ב	ד	ת	כ	
4	MEM	שׁ	כּ	ל	מ	
5	DALET	ה	ד	כ	ר	
6	KAF	כּ	ת	בּ	כ	
7	RESH	ד	ב	ר	ת	
8	CHAF	ה	ד	ת	כ	

OUR TRADITION – הַבְדָלָה

On Saturday night, after the first three stars can be seen in the sky, שַׁבָּת comes to an end. We have a special ceremony, called הַבְדָלָה, to separate שַׁבָּת from the new week.

הַבְדָלָה means "separation."

In the הַבְדָלָה ceremony we use a cup of wine, a braided candle, and a box filled with sweet spices. We hope that the coming week will be a good one.

What makes a week good?

Write or draw your answer here.

PICTURE PERFECT

Write the word שַׁבָּת below the two objects we can use to welcome שַׁבָּת.

Write the word הַבְדָלָה below the two objects we can use to say goodbye to שַׁבָּת.

LESSON 6

וְאָהַבְתָּ

And You Shall Love

LETTERS YOU KNOW. Say the name and sound of each letter.

בּ ת תּ שׁ מ ל כּ ה ר כ ב
ד

NEW LETTERS

א ו

VOWELS YOU KNOW. Say the sound of each vowel.

ַ ָ ְ ֲ

ALEF

1	אַ	אֲ	אָ	אֲ	אָ	אַ
2	אָ	שָׁ	לְ	הֲ	רָ	בְ
3	אֲ	הֲ	אָ	דָ	כְ	רְ

SHAPE IT UP

What does ***Alef*** look like?
Close your eyes and picture the letter.

Draw it in the air or use your whole body to make the shape of the letter ***Alef***.

Make up a clue to remember ***Alef***.

HEADS UP!

The letter א is always silent.
When it has a vowel under it, we say only the vowel sound.

READY, SET, READ

Read lines 1-4 while standing up. Read lines 5-8 while sitting down.

1 אָב   אַתְּ   אַל   אַשׁ   אָד   אָב

2 רָא   שְׁאָ   אַבָּ   אָמְ   אֲדָ   אָבְ

3 בָּא   כָּא   רָא   תָּא   הָאַ   אָהַ

4 אַתָּה   אֲדָר   כָּאַב   אָהַב   אָמַר   אֲבָל

5 בָּרָא   רָאָה   שָׁאַל   שְׁאָר   אַבָּא   שָׁאַב

6 שָׁאַבְתָּ   רָאֲתָה   אָכְלָה   שָׁאֲלָה   אָמְרָה

7 אָמַרְתָּ   אָכַלְתָּ   מַאֲכָל   בָּרָאתָ   אָכַלְתְּ

8 אָהַבְתָּ   אֲדָמָה   אַהֲבָה   אָבְדָה   אַהֲבָה

I KNOW HEBREW!

Can you find the Hebrew word above?

love = אַהֲבָה

Read it and circle or highlight it.

EXTRA CREDIT

Name the letters in the Hebrew word for ***love***.

NAME TAG

Read the name of the Hebrew letter in each box. Circle or highlight its matching Hebrew letter. What sound does the letter make?

ה	ד	ל	מ	LAMED	1
ת	ה	ב	ר	HAY	2
כ	ת	ד	ב	VET	3
מ	ל	כּ	שׁ	MEM	4
א	ת	ד	ה	ALEF	5
ר	כ	ד	ה	DALET	6
כ	בּ	תּ	כּ	KAF	7
ת	ר	ב	ד	RESH	8

VAV

וָ	וַ	וְ	וְ	וַ	וָ	1
הֲ	כְ	רְ	בַ	דְ	אֲ	2
דְ	רַ	בְ	בַ	וַ	וָ	3

SHAPE IT UP

What does ***Vav*** look like? Close your eyes and picture the letter.

Draw it in the air or use your whole body to make the shape of the letter ***Vav***.

Make up a clue to remember ***Vav***.

HEADS UP!

The letter ב and ו make the same sound.

What sound do they make?

READY, SET, READ

Read the odd-numbered lines in a funny voice.
Then read the even-numbered lines with an angry voice.

1 דָוַ שָׁוָ תָּוָ שְׁוָ וָלָ וְהָ

2 וָו וָה וַת וַר וַדָ וָאָ

3 לָוָ מַוָ כְּוַ הָוָ תָּו בַּוְ

4 דָוַר שָׁוָה תָּוָה אַוָה לָו אָבָה

5 אֲתַר דָוָה הָוָה שְׁוָא וָלָד דְבַשׁ

6 אֲשָׁרָה אַדְוָה רַאֲוָה וְאַתָּה וְאָהַב

7 אָבְדָה שַׁלְוָה וְאָכַל מְלַוָה הַדָבָר

8 וְהָלַכְתָּ וְאָהַבְתָּ וְאָמַרְתָּ וְלָמַדְתָּ וְאָהַבְתָּ

I KNOW HEBREW!

Can you find this Hebrew word above?

and you shall love = וְאָהַבְתָּ

Read it and circle or highlight it.

EXTRA CREDIT

On what line does וְאָהַבְתָּ appear?

___

WRITING PRACTICE

א

ו

Write the Hebrew word for ***love***.

אַהֲבָה

Write the Hebrew word for ***and you shall love***.

וְאָהַבְתָּ

How did you do? Circle your best ***Alef*** and your best ***Vav*** above.

WORD BUBBLES

With your eyes shut, point to a spot on the page.
Read aloud the word closest to where your finger lands.

Add the number in the circle to your score. Do it three times and see how high you can score.
Play with a partner and see who scores higher.

1 בְּרָכָה	2 הַבְדָּלָה	3 הַדָּבָר
2 אַהֲבָה	3 וְאָמַרְתָּ	1 וְאָהַב
3 וְאָהַבְתָּ	1 וְאַתָּה	2 אָמְרָה

OUR TRADITION — וְאָהַבְתָּ

וְאָהַבְתָּ means "and you shall love."
The Torah teaches us "to love God with all your heart, and with all your soul, and with all your might."

We call this teaching the וְאָהַבְתָּ and recite it during services in synagogue.

We also write the וְאָהַבְתָּ on a piece of parchment that is put inside the mezuzah and hung on the doorposts of our homes.

Why do you think the teaching "love God with all your heart, and with all your soul, and with all your might" is inside a mezuzah?

SHOW WHAT YOU KNOW

Complete the sentences below using Hebrew words from the word bank.

שַׁבָּת	וְאָהַבְתָּ	בְּרָכָה
שַׁמָּשׁ	הַבְדָּלָה	כַּלָּה

We welcome ____________ by saying a ____________ over candles.

We use the ______________ to light the candles on the Hanukkah menorah.

The special ceremony at the end of Shabbat is called ________________.

LESSON 7

צְדָקָה

Justice

NEW LETTERS

צ ק

LETTERS YOU KNOW. Say the name and sound of each letter.

בּ ת תּ שׁ מ ל כּ ה ו ר כ ב

ד א ו

VOWELS YOU KNOW. Say the sound of each vowel.

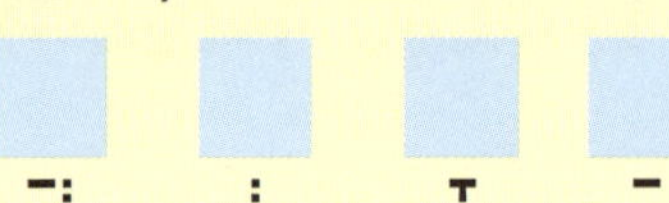

ַ ָ ְ ֲ

KOOF

ק

1	קַ	קְ	ק	קָ	קְ	קַ
2	קַ	רַ	כְּ	קְ	כְ	וְ
3	קַ	קְ	כַּ	כְּ	הֲ	אֲ

SHAPE IT UP

What does ***Koof*** look like?
Close your eyes and picture the letter.
Draw it in the air or use your whole body to make the shape of the letter ***Koof***.

Make up a clue to remember ***Koof***.

HEADS UP!

The letters ק and כּ make the same sound.

What sound do they make?

READY, SET, READ

Read all the words that start with a ***Koof***. Then read all the words that end with a ***Koof***. Find and read all the words that don't start or end with a ***Koof***.

1	קְרָ	קָשָׁ	קָבַ	קָדַ	וְקָ	קַבָּ
2	קָא	קַל	קַר	קַשׁ	קַו	קָה
3	בַּק	שַׁק	רַק	אָק	דַק	לָק
4	קָהָל	קָרָא	קָרָה	קָשָׁה	קָדַר	קָשַׁר
5	מָרָק	קְרָב	קַלָה	קָבַר	שָׁקַד	קָרַב
6	הֲרָקָה	כְּבָרָה	דַוְקָה	קָשַׁרְתְּ	קַבָּלָה	
7	מַמְתָּק	שָׁקַלְתָּ	בַּקָשָׁה	בְּבַקָשָׁה	הַבְרָקָה	
8	קַבָּלַת	שַׁבָּת	קַבָּלַת	שַׁבָּת	בְּבַקָשָׁה	

Great job!

I KNOW HEBREW!

Can you find these Hebrew words above?

Welcoming Shabbat = קַבָּלַת שַׁבָּת

please = בְּבַקָשָׁה

Read then circle or highlight them.

LETTER BOXES

Say the name of the Hebrew letter in each box. Circle or point to the sound each letter makes.

Sounds	Letter
V M R	מ
K CH L	ק
H V T	ה
T L SH	ל
V H M	ו
R K D	ד

TZADEE

1 צַ צְ צָ צ צַ צְ

2 קַ צַ קְ כְּ צְ לְ

3 צַ צְ קַ קְ כְּ דְ

SHAPE IT UP

What does ***Tzadee*** look like?
Close your eyes and picture the letter.

Draw it in the air or use your whole body to make the shape of the letter ***Tzadee***.

Make up a clue to remember ***Tzadee***.

HEADS UP!

The letter ***Tzadee*** makes a special sound.

Say the words ***Matzah Pizza***.

The middle sound in those two words is the sound of ***Tzadee***.

READY, SET, READ

Read lines 1-3 in a strong voice. Read lines 4-6 in a quiet voice. Read lines 7-8 in your regular voice.

צַו צָב צַר צַד צָה צָל 1

כְּצַ בָּצַ אָצָ מַצָ קָצַ רָצָ 2

אָכָה צָדַק כְּצַד בָּצַר אָצָה צָרָה 3

צָבָא צָבַּר קָצַר צְבָת בָּצָל מָצָא 4

מַצָה קְצַת קַצָב מַצָב הַצָב אָצַר 5

מָצָא צָלָה צָמַד מַצָה אָצְתָּ צָמָא 6

וְרָצָה וְאָצַר צָרַמְתְּ צַוָאר צָוְאָה 7

צְדָקָה בָּצַרְתָּ מָצָאתָ צָדַקְתָּ צְדָקָה 8

Which words were extra challenging? Practice reading them with a partner.

I KNOW HEBREW!

Can you find the Hebrew word above?

justice = צְדָקָה

Read it and circle or highlight it.

EXTRA CREDIT

Each year at Passover we eat a special food instead of bread.

Find the name of that food above, then read it aloud. What letter is in the middle of the word?

WORD BUBBLES

With your eyes shut, point to a spot on the page.
Read aloud the word closest to where your finger lands.

Add the number in the circle to your score. Do it three times and see how high you can score.
Play with a partner and see who scores higher.

POWER READING

Read aloud each line without making a mistake. Have a partner time you. How did you do?
Circle or highlight the word that was the most challenging.

1	צָרַמְתְּ	רָצְתָה	צָדְקָה	מָצָאתָ
2	בָּכְתָה	לָבַשְׁתְּ	שָׁאֲלָה	אָצַרְתָּ
3	הַבְדָּלָה	בְּבַקָּשָׁה	מְלָאכָה	הַקְדָשָׁה

WRITING PRACTICE

ק

צ

Write the Hebrew word for ***welcoming Shabbat***.

קַבָּלַת שַׁבָּת

Write the Hebrew word for ***matzah***.

מַצָּה

Write the Hebrew word for ***justice***..

צְדָקָה

How did you do? Circle your best ***Koof*** and your best ***Tzadee*** above.

WHAT'S MISSING?

Use the letters above each column to complete the four words in that column.
Read and translate each word.

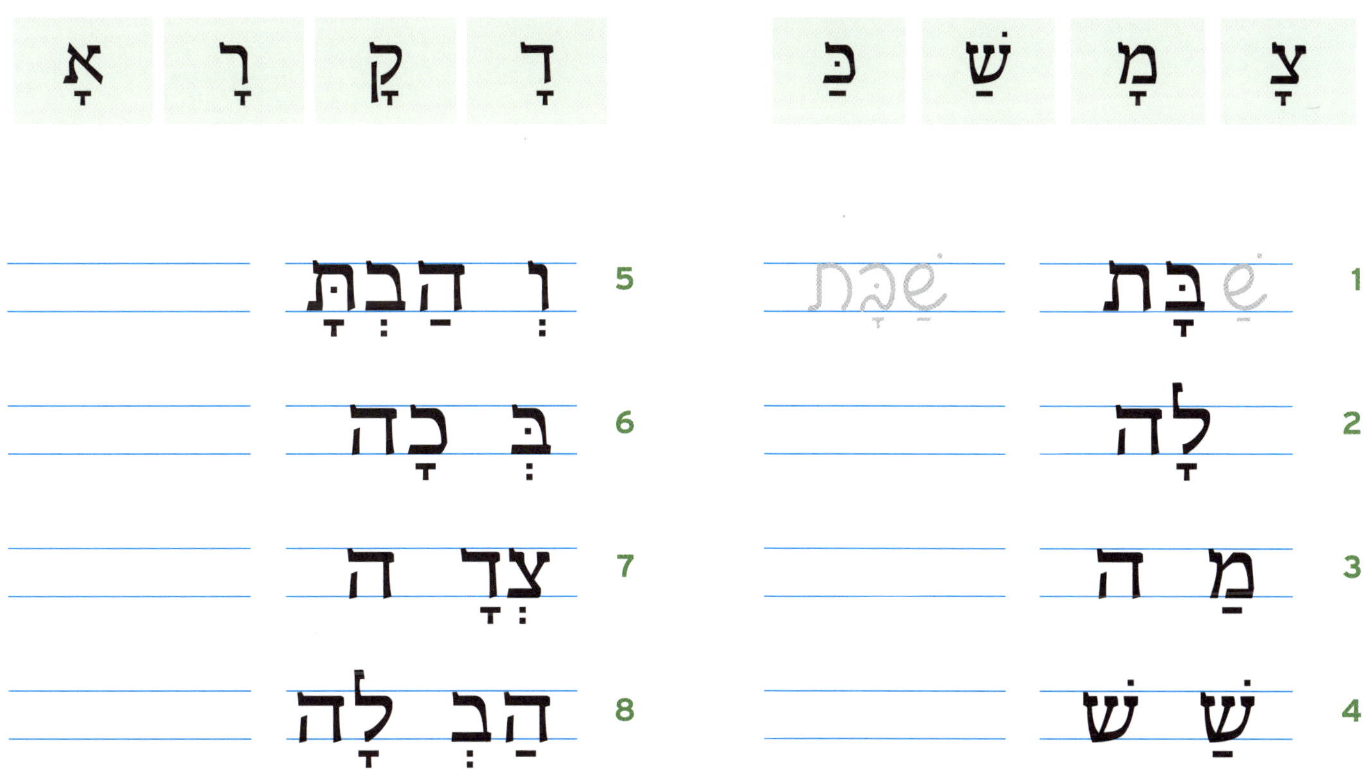

OUR TRADITION — צְדָקָה

צְדָקָה means "justice."

When we help other people improve their lives, we make the world more just and fair. The Torah teaches us that it is our responsibility to perform acts of צְדָקָה, acts of justice to help others. One way is to donate money to an organization that helps needy people.

Think of a time when you performed an act of צְדָקָה. Write about it or draw a picture of it here.

WORD MATCH

Match each Hebrew word with its English meaning. Read each Hebrew-English match aloud.

BLESSING	שַׁמָּשׁ
HELPER	בְּרָכָה
JUSTICE	הַבְדָּלָה
BRIDE	שַׁבָּת
SEPARATION	צְדָקָה
SHABBAT	כַּלָּה

CHECKPOINT CHALLENGE

Show off your Hebrew reading skills!

Choose a word for a partner to read. Then have your partner choose a word for you to read. Give yourself one point for every word read correctly. Can you get all 15?

1	אַהֲבָה	2	בְּרָכָה	3	דָבָר
4	דְרָשָׁה	5	הַבְדָלָה	6	וְאָהַבְתָּ
7	כַּלָה	8	הֲלָכָה	9	לָמַדְתָּ
10	מַצָה	11	צְדָקָה	12	קַבָּלַת
13	רַבָּה	14	שַׁבָּת	15	תָּו

ALEF BET CHART

You have learned eight new letters in Lessons 4-7:

ר כ ב ד א ו ק צ

Turn to the ***Alef Bet*** chart on page 160. Color in the new letters.

How many letters do you now know?

Can you name each letter?

LESSON 8

מִצְוָה

Commandment

NEW VOWELS

ִי ִ

LETTERS YOU KNOW. Say the name and sound of each letter.

בּ ת תּ שׁ מ ל כּ ה ר כ ב
ד א ו ק צ

VOWELS YOU KNOW. Say the sound of each vowel.

ַ ָ ְ ֲ

ִי ִ

1	בִּ	תִּ	מִ	הִ	וִ	אִ
2	דִי	כִ	רִ	כִּי	לִי	צִ
3	וִי	מִי	לִי	כִּי	בִּי	אִי

Which Hebrew sound reminds you of a buzzing insect? Circle or highlight it above.

SHAPE IT UP

What does ִ sound like?
Make a hand motion to show the shape of ִ as you say its sound.

What does ִי sound like?
Make a hand motion to show the shape of ִי as you say its sound.

READY, SET, READ

Read lines 1-4. Then, take a break. Stand up and stretch your body. Read lines 5-8.

1 מִק צַדִּי לְבִי אֲוִי דָוִ בְּרִי

2 שִׁשָּׁה הִכָּה בִּיב שְׁמִי צִיר הֲכִי

3 הִיא אִישׁ אִשָּׁה אִמָּא בְּכִי בְּלִי

4 רַבִּי אֲוִיר דָוִד בִּימָה דָתִי תִּיק

5 שִׁירָה תִּירָא רִמָּה קְרִיאַת לְבִיבָה קָצִיר

6 צַדִּיק בְּרִיאַת קַדִּישׁ אָבִיב קְהִלָּה מִקְרָא

7 צִיצִית בְּרִית מִילָה תִּקְוָה הַתִּקְוָה

8 מִצְוָה הַמִּצְוָה בַּר מִצְוָה בַּת מִצְוָה

I KNOW HEBREW!

Can you find the Hebrew words above?
Read and circle or highlight them.

commandment = מִצְוָה

bar mitzvah = בַּר מִצְוָה

bat mitzvah = בַּת מִצְוָה

knotted fringes on the corners of the tallit = צִיצִית

Kaddish = קַדִּישׁ

"The Hope", the national anthem of Israel = הַתִּקְוָה

Mommy = אִמָּא

A Hebrew speaker may call their mother אִמָּא.

Write the Hebrew word for "mother." ______________

WRITING PRACTICE

Write the Hebrew word for ***commandment***.

מִצְוָה מִצְוָה

Write the Hebrew word for ***bar mitzvah***.

בַּר מִצְוָה בַּר מִצְוָה

Write the Hebrew word for ***bat mitzvah***.

בַּת מִצְוָה בַּת מִצְוָה

Write the Hebrew word for ***fringes on the corners of the tallit.***

צִיצִית צִיצִית

Write the Hebrew word for ***Kaddish***..

קַדִּישׁ קַדִּישׁ

Write the Hebrew word for ***the Hope, the national anthem of Israel.***

הַתִּקְוָה הַתִּקְוָה

RHYME TIME

Read the Hebrew words below.

Connect the rhyming words, then sing them out loud.

1	בַּר	מִצְוָה
2	מִקְוָה	אָדִישׁ
3	דִּבְּרָה	קְרִיאַת
4	קַדִּישׁ	אַבִּיר
5	קָצִיר	כַּר
6	בְּרִיאַת	מִקְרָא

OUR TRADITION – מִצְוָה

A מִצְוָה is a commandment from God. These commandments are written in the Torah.

We do a מִצְוָה when we light Shabbat candles, hear the shofar on Rosh Hashanah, honor our parents, feed our pets, or visit a sick friend.

What is a מִצְוָה you have done? Write about it or draw it here.

WORD WIZARD

Read aloud each line. Find the Hebrew letter that is found in every word on the line. Write it on the line.

1	מַלְבִּישׁ	רַבִּי	מִדְבָּר	דִּבְּרָה	______
2	אִירָא	בְּקִרְבִּי	בְּרִית	מִדְרָשׁ	______
3	תָּמִיד	מָרָה	בִּימָה	אָמַרְתִּי	______
4	מַצִּיל	צְדָקָה	צִיצִית	מִצְוָה	______
5	הַתִּקְוָה	אָבִיו	צִוָּה	בְּשַׁלְוִי	______
6	לְהָבִיא	אִשָּׁה	אָהַבְתִּי	קְהִילָּה	______

Write the six letters from these lines below.

______	______	______	______	______	______
6	5	4	3	2	1

What does this mean?

LESSON 9

שְׁמַע

Hear

NEW LETTER

ע

LETTERS YOU KNOW. Say the name and sound of each letter.

בּ ת תּ שׁ מ ל כּ ה ר כ ב

ד א ו ק צ

VOWELS YOU KNOW. Say the sound of each vowel.

◌ַ ◌ָ ◌ְ ◌ֲ ◌ִ ◌ִי

AYIN

1	עַ	עָ	עֲ	עִ	עִי	עָ
2	עַ	אַ	הַ	עֲ	אֲ	הֲ
3	עִי	צִי	קִי	אֲ	הֲ	עֲ

SHAPE IT UP

What does ***Ayin*** look like?
Close your eyes and picture the letter.

Draw it in the air or use your whole body to make the shape of the letter ***Ayin***.

Make up a clue to remember ***Ayin***.

HEADS UP!

The letter ע does not have its own sound.

When it has a vowel under it, we say only the vowel sound.

What other letter doesn't have its own sound?

READY, SET, READ

Read line 1 softly, then read line 2 loudly. Continue alternating how you read each line. Then read the lines again, this time reading the odd-numbered lines loudly and the even-numbered lines softly.

1 עָשִׂי עָתִי עָבַ צָעִי מַע דַעַ

2 עַל עָבָ עַד רַע עִיר עַר

3 וַעַד דַעַת עַתָּה רַעַשׁ בַּעַל עָבַר

4 שְׁמַע רָעָב צָעִיר תָּקַע עִמָה שָׁעָה

5 רָקִיעַ עָתִיד עָשִׂיר אַרְבַּע עַתִיק עִבְרִי

6 עִבְרִית מַעֲרִיב תְּקִיעָה עֲמִידָה קְעָרָה

7 שַׁעֲוָה עָבַדְתִּי שִׁבְעָה עֲתִיקָה עֲמִידָה

8 שְׁמַע תִּשְׁמַע שְׁמִיעָה קְרִיאַת שְׁמַע

I KNOW HEBREW!

Can you find this Hebrew word above?

hear = שְׁמַע

Read it loudly so that others can ***hear*** you.

Can you find this Hebrew word above?

Hebrew = עִבְרִית

What letter does it start with?

What letter does it end with?

POWER READING

Read aloud each line without making a mistake. Have a partner time you. How did you do? Circle or highlight the word that was the most challenging.

1	צַעַד	לָמַד	שָׁעָה	בַּעַל
2	בָּקַע	עָמַד	שַׁעַר	שָׁעַל
3	בְּרַעַשׁ	בִּשְׁעַת	עֲרִירִי	הִשְׁמִיעַ
4	עֲמִידָה	וְעָצַר	עָבַדְתָּ	עָמְדָה
5	וְדִבַּרְתָּ	וְאָהַבְתָּ	לְהַקְדִּישׁ	אַרְבָּעָה
6	וְעָבַדְתָּ	וְהָאֲדָמָה	וְאָמַרְתָּ	וְאָכַלְתָּ

SOUNDS LIKE

Clap your hands as you read aloud each Hebrew word on the first line.

Circle or highlight the word on each line that sounds the same as the Hebrew in the box. Then compare your answer with a partner's.

1	צַו	עָב	רַב	צָב
2	קָרָא	רָקַע	קָרַע	צָבָא
3	אִמָא	עִמָא	צָמָא	אִתָּה
4	עָשִׁיר	אֲוִיר	עָתִיד	אָשִׁיר
5	מַצָה	צַעַד	מָצָא	צַמָה
6	דָבָר	הֲדַר	דַוָר	הָדָד

WRITING PRACTICE

How did you do? Circle your best ***Ayin*** above.

WORD BUBBLES

With your eyes shut, point to a spot on the page.
Read aloud the word closest to where your finger lands.

Add the number in the circle to your score. Do it three times and see how high you can score.
Play with a partner and see who scores higher.

3 וְאָהַבְתָּ	2 שְׁמַע	1 מַצָּה
2 הַתִּקְוָה	3 עֲמִידָה	1 צִיצִית
3 מַעֲרִיב	1 תְּקִיעָה	2 צַדִּיק

OUR TRADITION – שְׁמַע

The Hebrew word שְׁמַע means "hear."

שְׁמַע is the first word and the name of one of our most important prayers. The words of שְׁמַע come from the Torah. When we recite the שְׁמַע, we are saying we believe in One God—"Hear O Israel, Adonai is Our God, Adonai is One."

Why do you think we need to tell everyone to hear us? Why can't we just say this in our hearts or to ourselves?

Hand motions can help us think more about the words we say. What hand motions would you do when reciting the שְׁמַע? Write or draw them here.

PICTURE PERFECT

Read each word.

Write the correct word below the matching picture.

צְדָקָה

שְׁמַע

עִבְרִית

כַּלָּה

צִיצִית

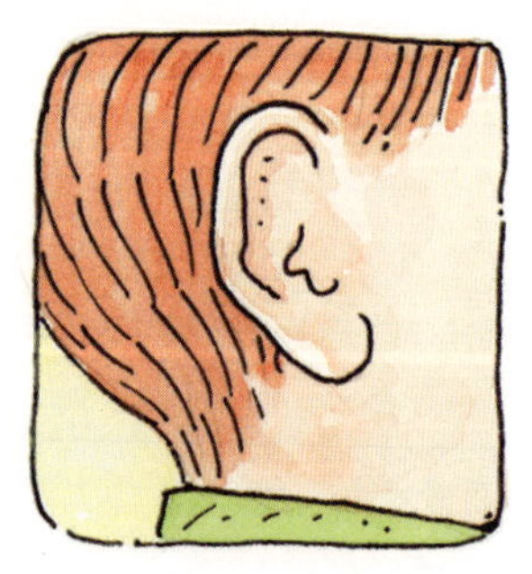

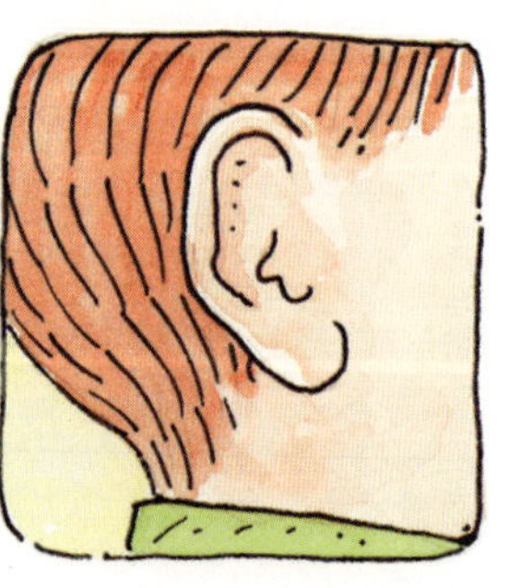

LESSON 10

נָבִיא

Prophet

NEW LETTERS

ן נ

LETTERS YOU KNOW. Say the name and sound of each letter.

בּ ת תּ שׁ מ ל כּ ה ר כ ב

ד א ו ק צ ע

VOWELS YOU KNOW. Say the sound of each vowel.

◌ַ ◌ָ ◌ְ ◌ֲ ◌ִ ◌ִי

FINAL NUN/NUN

1	נַ	נָ	נִי	נְ	נִ	נְ
2	נִ	נִי	עִי	וִי	רִ	בִ
3	לָן	דָן	מִין	רָן	מִן	כַּן

Which Hebrew sound reminds you of a part of your body?

SHAPE IT UP

What do ***Nun*** and ***Final Nun*** look like?

Close your eyes and picture the letters.

Draw them in the air or use your whole body to make the shapes of the letters ***Nun*** and ***Final Nun***.

Make up clues to remember ***Nun*** and ***Final Nun***.

HEADS UP!

There are five letters of the Hebrew alphabet that have a different form when they come at the end of a word.

When a נ comes at the end of a word, it is a ***Final*** ן.

READY, SET, READ

Read lines 1-3 in a happy 🙂 voice. Read lines 4-5 in a sad 🙁 voice.
Read lines 6-8 in your regular voice.

1	נָן	נָו	נְעִי	קַן	בִּין	
2	נִין	לָן	דָן	מָן	שִׁין	רָן
3	דִין	בְּנִי	עָנִי	נָקִי	אֲנִי	נָא
4	שָׁנָה	לָבָן	עָנָו	רִנָה	עָנַד	נַעַר
5	נָבִיא	בִּינָה	נְשָׁמָה	מִשְׁנָה	נְעָרָה	
6	מַאֲמִין	שְׁכִינָה	כַּוָנָה	נְעִילָה	מַרְבִּין	
7	רַעֲנָן	מִשְׁכָּן	לְהָבִין	קַנְקַן	לַמְדָן	
8	נָבִיא	מְדִינָה	מַה	נִשְׁתַּנָה	נָבִיא	

I KNOW HEBREW!

Can you find the Hebrew word above?

prophet = נָבִיא

Read it and circle or highlight it.

EXTRA CREDIT

At the Passover seder, the youngest child asks the Four Questions.

Can you find the two Hebrew words in the lines above that introduce the Four Questions? Read them.

If you remember the tune to the Four Questions, sing the first line!

I SPY

Read aloud each line.

Find the Hebrew that sounds the same as the English in the box. Write the two Hebrew sounds on the line.

1	AH	הֲ	אֲ	צַ	תַ	עָ	אֲ	עָ
2	DEE	רִי	הִי	דִיא	דִי	רְ		
3	VAH	נָא	בַ	כַ	לָא	וָא		
4	KEE	כִּי	שִׁי	בִּ	קִי	תִּי		
5	HEE	אִי	הִיא	תִי	וִי	הִי		

SOUNDS LIKE

Stomp your foot as you read aloud each line. Which two Hebrew words sound the same? Circle them or show them to a partner.

1	מַה	מָן	מָנָה	מָא
2	נָא	וָנָא	נָע	נָוָה
3	לָבָן	לְבָנָה	לָוַן	לְנָוָה
4	עָנָו	אָנָא	עָנָן	אֲנָב
5	אָנִית	אֲנִי	עָנִי	עַנָת
6	כִּינַע	קָנָה	כַּוָנָה	קַבָנָא

WRITING PRACTICE

נ ן

ן ן

Write the Hebrew word for ***prophet***.

נָבִיא

Write the Hebrew word for ***Haman***.

הָמָן

Do you know who Haman was?

NUN ADD-IN

Complete each word below by adding the correct form of the letter ***Nun***.
Then read all the words. When you read the word that means ***prophet***, stand up.
When you read the word ***Haman***, boo loudly.

1 ָ___בִיא   2 נָתַ___   3 אֲ___ִי

4 הָמָ___   5 ___ְשָׁמָה   6 שָׁ___ָה

7 מַתָּ___ָה   8 כַּנָּ___ָה   9 לָבָ___

10 מִשְׁכָּ___   11 מַאֲמִי___   12 מַה ___ִשְׁתַּ___ָה

OUR TRADITION — נָבִיא

The Hebrew word נָבִיא means "prophet." In the days of the Bible a נָבִיא was a spokesperson for God. The נָבִיא gave hope to our people when they felt sad and lost. These are the names of some of our prophets: Joshua, Isaiah, Jeremiah, Ezekiel, Hosea, and Deborah. Our first and greatest נָבִיא was Moses.

Think about a time when you helped someone who felt sad or lost. Whom did you help? What did you say or do? Write about it or draw it here.

WORD POWER

Read aloud the Hebrew words on each line.
Circle or highlight the word that has the same meaning as the English in the box.

1	HEBREW	שָׁנָה	עִבְרִית	כַּוָּנָה	קְרִיאַת
2	PROPHET	שְׁכִינָה	מַעֲרִיב	אַרְבַּע	נָבִיא
3	AND YOU SHALL LOVE	נְשָׁמָה	תְּקִיעָה	וְאָהַבְתָּ	בְּרִית
4	COMMANDMENT	קַדִּישׁ	אִמָּא	אַהֲבָה	מִצְוָה
5	THE HOPE	קַבָּלַת	הַתִּקְוָה	מִשְׁכַּן	נְעִילָה

LESSON 11

Braided Bread

for Shabbat and holidays

LETTERS YOU KNOW. Say the name and sound of each letter.

בּ ת תּ שׁ מ ל כּ ה ר כ ב

ד א ו ק צ ע נ ן

VOWELS YOU KNOW. Say the sound of each vowel.

◌ַ ◌ָ ◌ְ ◌ֲ ◌ִ ◌ִי

NEW LETTER

CHET

1 חַ חִ חִי חֲ חָ ח

2 כַ חַ כִי חִי כָ חָ

3 חִי הִי חֲ הֲ חָ הָ

SHAPE IT UP

What does ***Chet*** look like?
Close your eyes and picture the letter.

Draw it in the air or use your whole body to make the shape of the letter ***Chet***.

Make up a clue to remember ***Chet***.

HEADS UP!

The letters ח and כ make the same sound.

What sound do these letters make?

READY, SET, READ

Read all the words that start with ***Chet***, and have a partner read all the words that end with ***Chet***. Together read the words that have ***Chet*** in the middle. Then whisper the words that do not have a ***Chet***.

1 חִכָּ חָבִי חָתָ בָּח אַח צָח

2 חָל חִיל חַד חָשׁ חִישׁ חִימִי

3 קַח צַח נָח לָח אָח חַוָה

4 חִכָּה שָׁכַח חָבִיב חֲבָל חָתָן לָקַח

5 חַלָה חָלִיל וְצָחַק אַחַת חָצִיר חָנָן

6 מִנְחָה חֲמִשָׁה שָׁלְחָה חִירִיק בָּחַרְתָּ

7 רַחֲמָן הָרַחֲמָן שַׁחֲרִית חֲתִימָה חֲדָשָׁה

8 הַחַלָה הַבְּרָכָה חַלָה לְשַׁבָּת הָרַחֲמָן

I KNOW HEBREW!

Can you find these Hebrew words above?

the Merciful One (God) = הָרַחֲמָן

braided bread = חַלָה

Read and circle or highlight them.

EXTRA CREDIT

How many times did you read the word for ***braided bread***?

LETTER AND VOWEL WORKOUT

You have learned all these letters and vowels!

Say the name of each letter in lines 1-18.

Take turns with a partner reading all the lines. As you do, choose a movement for each line. For example, scratch your head while reading line 1, or rub your hands together while reading line 2.

SOUNDS LIKE

Can you find the Hebrew that sounds like the English word for:

- A hot beverage?
- Something you use to open a lock?
- A buzzing insect?

Circle or highlight those sounds.

אִי	אִ	אֲ	אָ	אַ	1
בִּי	בִּ	בְּ	בָּ	בַּ	2
בִי	בִ	בְ	בָ	בַ	3
דִי	דִ	דְ	דָ	דַ	4
הִי	הִ	הֲ	הָ	הַ	5
וִי	וִ	וְ	וָ	וַ	6
חִי	חִ	חֲ	חָ	חַ	7
כִּי	כִּ	כְּ	כָּ	כַּ	8
כִי	כִ	כְ	כָ	כַ	9
לִי	לִ	לְ	לָ	לַ	10
מִי	מִ	מְ	מָ	מַ	11
נִי	נִ	נְ	נָ	נַ	12
עִי	עִ	עֲ	עָ	עַ	13
צִי	צִ	צְ	צָ	צַ	14
קִי	קִ	קְ	קָ	קַ	15
רִי	רִ	רְ	רָ	רַ	16
שִׁי	שִׁ	שְׁ	שָׁ	שַׁ	17
תִי	תִ	תְ	תָ	תַ	18

WRITING PRACTICE

ח ח ח

Write the Hebrew word for ***braided bread***.

חַלָּה חַלָּה חַלָּה

Write the Hebrew word for ***Merciful One (God)***.

הָרַחֲמָן הָרַחֲמָן הָרַחֲמָן

RHYME TIME

Read the words on each line. Three words on each line rhyme. Circle the word that does not rhyme and write it on the line. Now sing aloud the rhyming words.

1	צַח	קַח	לָדָה	אָח	לָדָה
2	חַלָּה	חָמָה	חָתָן	כַּלָּה	
3	אֲבֵדָה	חָבִיב	אָבִיב	מַעֲרִיב	
4	עִבְרִית	אָשִׁיר	שַׁחֲרִית	עַרְבִית	
5	תְּקִיעָה	קְרִיאָה	עֲמִידָה	הַנָּבִיא	
6	לָקַח	שָׁחַת	שָׁכַח	שָׁלַח	

OUR TRADITION – חַלָּה

חַלָּה is the braided bread we eat on שַׁבָּת. When we welcome שַׁבָּת, we recite a בְּרָכָה over חַלָּה, as well as over candles and wine.

Why do you think we eat special bread on Shabbat?

Close your eyes and imagine you're eating חַלָּה. How does it taste? What does it smell like?

EXTRA CREDIT

In a group, recite the בְּרָכָה we say over candles, wine, and חַלָּה when we welcome שַׁבָּת.

WORD SKILLS

Read the Hebrew words below. Write the correct Hebrew word above its English meaning. Read the sentence using the Hebrew word.

בְּרָכָה	חַלָּה	שְׁמַע
נָבִיא	צְדָקָה	מִצְוָה

1 We say a ______________ to say ***Thank You*** to God.
blessing

2 It is a ______________ to help feed the hungry.
mitzvah

3 We eat ______________ on שַׁבָּת.
braided bread

4 A ______________ was a spokesperson for God.
Prophet

5 We say the prayer ______________ ***O Israel, Adonai is our God, Adonai is One*** in the morning and evening.
hear

6 When we perform an act of ______________, we are following God's commandments.
justice

עֲלִיָה

Going Up

the honor of being called up to recite the blessings over the Torah

LETTERS YOU KNOW. Say the name and sound of each letter.

בּ ת תּ שׁ מ ל כּ ה ר כ ב

ד א ו ק צ ע נ ן ח

VOWELS YOU KNOW. Say the sound of each vowel.

ַ ָ ְ ֲ ִ ִי

NEW LETTER

י

YUD

1	יַ	יָ	יִי	יִ	יְ	יָ
2	יַ	וַ	יְ	וְ	יִי	וִי
3	יָשָׁ	יָר	יִן	יְשִׁי	חַי	יְדִי

SHAPE IT UP

What does ***Yud*** look like? Close your eyes and picture the letter.

Draw it in the air or use your whole body to make the shape of the letter ***Yud***.

Make up a clue to remember ***Yud***.

READY, SET, READ

Read aloud the lines below while standing on one foot. Switch to the other foot halfway.

1	יָד	יְהִי	יַיִן	יַמִי	יָדִי	יָמָה
2	שַׁיִשׁ	יָשָׁן	מִיָד	נְיָר	לַיִל	הֲיִי
3	בַּיִת	יָשָׁר	יַעַר	חַיָה	עַיִן	יָשַׁב
4	יָדַע	אַיִל	חַיָב	יָחִיד	יָקָר	מַעְיָן
5	יְצִיר	הָיָה	יָוָן	חַיִל	יָצָא	עֲדַיִן
6	יַחְדָו	יִרְאָה	יִצְחָק	יַבָּשָׁה	צִיַרְתִּי	
7	עֲלִיָה	כְּוִיָה	יִוָכַח	יַלְדָה	יְדִיעָה	
8	יְשִׁיבָה	יִשְׁתַּבַּח	הָיְתָה	מִנְיָן	עֲלִיָה	

I KNOW HEBREW!

Can you find these Hebrew words above?

***aliyah*, going up** = עֲלִיָה

***minyan*, ten Jewish adults, the minimum needed to recite some prayers** = מִנְיָן

Read and circle or highlight them.

EXTRA CREDIT

Can you find the word יָד above?

It is the Hebrew word for ***hand***.

It is also the word for the pointer used to touch the parchment of the Torah.

WRITING PRACTICE

י

Write the Hebrew word for ***aliyah, going up***.

עֲלִיָּה

Write the Hebrew word for ***minyan, ten Jewish adults***.

מִנְיָן

YUD DETECTIVE

Each word to the right contains at least one ***Yud***.

With a partner, take turns reading all the words that begin with ***Yud***. When your partner reads a word correctly, raise your יָד, your hand. Cross out or circle all the words read correctly.

Yud is the smallest letter in the Hebrew alphabet. Read in a small voice all the words that are left.

1 יַדְעָן שִׁירָה תְּחִיָּה יְמָמָה

2 עֲנִיבָה יַעֲנָה יַלְדָּה יִצְחָק

3 יָנַק יָקָר קְנִיָּה מַכִּיר

4 הִיא בְּנִי שִׁירָה בַּיִת

5 רִיב יַחַד קַמְתִּי נָדִיר

6 יְקָרָה חָבִיב עֲנִיבָה נָבִיא

7 יְדִיעָה יָצַב יַבָּשָׁה אַיִן

8 יָשַׁע יָשַׁבְתָּ עִנְיָן יָהִיר

9 עַיִן יָמִין יָרַשְׁתָּ רְצִינִי

EXTRA CREDIT

Circle any word that has a silent yud that is part of the vowel EE (ִי)

Write that word. ____________________

OUR TRADITION — עֲלִיָּה

In the synagogue, the honor of being called up to the Torah is known as an עֲלִיָּה. The word עֲלִיָּה means "going up." We go up to the *bimah* and recite blessings before and after each section of the Torah is read.

The word עֲלִיָּה also has another meaning. If someone moves to Israel, that person is making עֲלִיָּה, because they are going up to the land of Israel, the Holy Land.

Have you ever seen someone being called up for an עֲלִיָּה?
Did the person look nervous, proud, excited, or something else? How would you feel?

CONNECTIONS

Read the word parts in each column.

Connect the beginning of a word in the right column to its ending in the left column.

Read each word aloud.

1	שַׁ	וָה
2	הַבְ	הַבְתָּ
3	בְּרָ	יָן
4	וְאָ	דָלָה
5	צְדָ	בָּת
6	מִצְ	יָה
7	מִנְ	קָה
8	עֲלִ	כָה

To Life

NEW LETTER

ם

LETTERS YOU KNOW. Say the name and sound of each letter.

בּ ת תּ שׁ מ ל כּ ה ר כ ב

ד א ו ק צ ע נ ן ח י

VOWELS YOU KNOW. Say the sound of each vowel.

ַ ָ ֲ ְ ִ ִי

FINAL MEM

ם

1	תָּם	קָם	צָם	דָם	אִם	חַם
2	עַם	שָׁם	יָם	בָּם	רָם	עִם
3	יִים	תִּים	רַיִם	לִים	הָם	אִים

SHAPE IT UP

What does ***Final Mem*** look like?
Close your eyes and picture the letter.
Draw it in the air or use your whole body to make the shape of the letter ***Final Mem***.

Make up a clue to remember ***Final Mem***.

HEADS UP!

There are five letters in the Hebrew alphabet that have a different form when they come at the end of a word.

When a מ comes at the end of a word, it is a ***Final*** ם.

What other letter have you learned that has a different form at the end of a word?

Write that letter here: ______________.

Write that letter in its final form here: ______________.

READY, SET, READ

Read aloud each line. When you read a word that ends in the sound "eem," stand up. When you read a word that ends in "ahm," sit down.

1 הָלַם אַחִים עָלִים מִרְיָם בַּדִים תָּרַם

2 אִיים שְׁנַיִם בָּתִּים אָדָם דַקִים מִצְרַיִם

3 חָכָם רַעַם יָמִים רַבִּים חַיִים דָמַם

4 בָּנִים מַיִם אָדָם שְׁתַּיִם מִלִים אָשָׁם

5 נָשִׁים שָׁמַיִם דְבָרִים יָדַיִם קָמִים עָלִים

6 אַבְרָהָם נְבִיאִים כְּרָמִים שִׁבְעִים אֲנָשִׁים

7 עִבְרִים רַחֲמִים יְלָדִים צַדִיקִים מְלָכִים

8 עֲבָדִים יְצִיאַת מִצְרַיִם לְחַיִים לְחַיִים

I KNOW HEBREW!

Can you find these Hebrew words above?

to life = לְחַיִים

the name of the first human in the Torah = אָדָם

the Exodus, going out from Egypt = יְצִיאַת מִצְרַיִם

Read and circle or highlight them.

WORD BUBBLES

With your eyes shut, point to a spot on the page. Read the word closest to where your finger lands.

Add the number in the circle to your score. Do it three times and see how high you can score. Play with a partner and see who scores higher.

Want a higher score? Earn one point for each word translated correctly.

VOCABULARY CHALLENGE

You know the English meaning of many of the words in the ***Word Bubbles*** activity above. Read the Hebrew and give the English meaning for the words you know.

WRITING PRACTICE

ם

Write the Hebrew word for ***the first human in the Torah***.

אָדָם

Write the Hebrew word for ***To Life!***

לְחַיִּים

Write the Hebrew words for ***Exodus from Egypt***.

יְצִיאַת מִצְרַיִם

HEADS UP!

מ and ם have the same sound. How are they different?

Make up a clue to help you remember the difference between מ and ם.

____

Complete each word by adding the correct form of ***Mem***.

Read the words to a partner. Do you know the meanings of some of the words?

How many?________

1 שְׁנַיִ__	2 הָ__ָ__ן	3 שְׁ__ַע
4 הָרַחֲ__ָן	5 אַבְרָהָ__	6 בִּרְכַּיִ__
7 לְחַיִּי__	8 יַ__ִי__	9 __ִצְוָה
10 __ִנְיָן	11 אָדָ__	12 __ִצְרַיִם

OUR TRADITION – לְחַיִּים

לְחַיִּים means “to life.” At a special celebration, such as a wedding or graduation, it is traditional to clink our glasses together and say לְחַיִּים!

The word חַיִּים means “life” and appears in many of our prayers.

When would you say לְחַיִּים? Write about it or draw it here.

Read aloud the Hebrew words on each line.
Circle or highlight the word that has the same meaning as the English in the box.

1	BLESSING	בְּרָכָה	חַלָּה	הַבְדָּלָה	שַׁמָּשׁ
2	TO LIFE	מִצְוָה	חָכָם	עֲבָדִים	לַחַיִּים
3	HEAR	נָבִיא	בָּנִים	שְׁמַע	שְׁתַּיִם
4	GOING UP	מִצְרַיִם	עֲלִיָּה	עַיִן	יְצִיאַת
5	JUSTICE	יְלָדִים	שָׁמַיִם	צְדָקָה	יְשִׁיבָה

CHECKPOINT CHALLENGE

Show off your Hebrew reading skills! Choose a word for your partner to read. Then have your partner choose a word for you to read. Give yourself one point for every word read correctly. Continue until you have read all the words.

צַדִיק	4	נָבִיא	3	רַבִּי	2	אִמָא	1
לַחַיִים	8	אָחִי	7	דָוִד	6	יְהִי	5
מִצְוָה	12	עֲלִיָה	11	לְכִי	10	כִּי	9
צִיצִית	16	עִבְרִית	15	נִין	14	אֲנִי	13
הַתִּקְוָה	20	שִׁירָה	19	בְּרִית	18	תְּקִיעָה	17

Which box contains the boy's name David? ______________

ALEF BET CHART

You have learned six new letters in Lessons 9-13:

ע נ ן ח י ם

Turn to the ***Alef Bet*** chart on page 160. Color in the new letters. Can you say the name and sound of each letter you now know?

LESSON 14

תּוֹרָה

Torah, Teaching

NEW VOWELS

ֹ וֹ

LETTERS YOU KNOW. Say the name and sound of each letter.

בּ ת תּ שׁ מ ל כּ ה ר כ ב

ד א ו ק צ ע נ ן ח י ם

VOWELS YOU KNOW. Say the sound of each vowel.

ַ ָ ְ ֲ ִ ִי

ֹ וֹ

1 תּוֹ בּוֹ רוֹ מוֹ לוֹ דוֹ נוֹ

2 אֹ צֹ קֹ עֹ נֹ חֹ יֹ

3 מֹעַ עוֹת אָנֹ שׁוֹן קֹב דוֹשׁ

SHAPE IT UP

What does וֹ sound like? Make a hand motion to show the shape of וֹ as you say its sound.

What does ֹ sound like? Make a hand motion to show the shape of ֹ as you say its sound.

Look at lines 1-3 above. What sounds like:

The opposite of "yes"? Write it in Hebrew here: ____________

The opposite of "high"? Write it in Hebrew here: ____________

HEADS UP!

Usually a vowel is found below a letter: רִ, שַׁ.

But the vowel וֹ or ֹ comes after a letter: תּוֹ מֹ.

READY, SET, READ

Read aloud the odd-numbered lines. Read aloud the even-numbered lines.

1 כֹל לֹא אוֹת יוֹם חוֹל צֹאן

2 עוֹד קוֹל מוֹת שׁוֹר צוֹם חוֹר

3 שָׁמַע יָבֹא אֹתָם דָתוֹ אָנֹכִי כְּמוֹ

4 אָבוֹת מְאֹד כָּבוֹד לָשׁוֹן נָכוֹן שָׁעוֹת

5 קָדוֹשׁ תּוֹרָה צִיוֹן מוֹרָה תְּהֹם מְלֹא

6 שְׁלֹמֹה אַהֲרֹן יַעֲקֹב אֲדוֹן עוֹלָם

7 הַמּוֹצִיא שַׁבָּת שָׁלוֹם רֹאשׁ הַשָּׁנָה

8 תּוֹרָה בְּרָכוֹת מִצְווֹת דּוֹרוֹת כֹּהֲנִים

How did you do? Choose four words that were challenging to read. Read them again to a partner.

I KNOW HEBREW!

Can you find these Hebrew words above?
Circle or point to them. Then read each word.

Torah, teaching = תּוֹרָה

Holy = קָדוֹשׁ

Hello, goodbye, peace = שָׁלוֹם

A peaceful Shabbat = שַׁבָּת שָׁלוֹם

Blessing over bread = הַמּוֹצִיא

Jewish New Year = רֹאשׁ הַשָּׁנָה

EXTRA CREDIT

Can you find the name of the ***Jewish New Year*** in the words above?

Write it here.________________

Can you recite the בְּרָכָה we say over חַלָּה?

WORD BUBBLES

With your eyes shut, point to a spot on the page. Read the word closest to where your finger lands.

Add the number in the circle to your score. Do it three times and see how high you can score. Play with a partner and see who scores higher.

Want a higher score? Earn one point for each word translated correctly.

1 עֲלִיָּה

2 מִנְיָן

3 עוֹלָם

2 נְשָׁמָה

1 שָׁלוֹם

3 כַּוָּנָה

1 בְּרִית

2 תּוֹרָה

3 שַׁחֲרִית

1 שְׁמַע

WORD RIDDLE

My name means "peace." It also means "hello" and "goodbye."

My name contains the vowel וֹ.

Who am I?

WRITING PRACTICE

Write the Hebrew words for ***a peaceful Shabbat***.

שַׁבָּת שָׁלוֹם

Write the Hebrew word for the ***blessing over bread***.

הַמּוֹצִיא

Write the Hebrew words for the ***Jewish New Year***.

רֹאשׁ הַשָּׁנָה

Write the Hebrew word for ***Torah***.

תּוֹרָה

Write the Hebrew word for ***holy***.

קָדוֹשׁ

Write the Hebrew word for ***hello***, ***goodbye***, and ***peace***.

שָׁלוֹם

RHYME TIME

Read the words on each line and find the three that rhyme. Then, sing the rhyming words aloud.

1	בַּר	קַר	הַר	בַּת
2	שׁוֹר	חוֹם	חוֹר	תּוֹר
3	תּוֹרָה	לִקְרֹא	אוֹרָה	מוֹרָה
4	לָשׁוֹן	שָׁעוֹן	עוֹלָם	נָכוֹן
5	קָדוֹשׁ	רֹאשׁ	שָׁלוֹשׁ	רוֹצָה
6	דּוֹר	חוֹל	קוֹל	הַכֹּל
7	אוֹתוֹ	חַיּוֹת	שְׁנוֹת	בְּרִיּוֹת
8	שָׁלוֹם	אָדוֹם	חַלּוֹת	חֲלוֹם

EXTRA CREDIT

The Hebrew word for the number three starts and ends with the same letter, שׁ.

Can you find it above?

Read all the words on that line.

WORD RIDDLE

I am a word repeated three times in a row when we recite the עֲמִידָה.
I mean "holy." I begin with the letter ק. Who am I?

OUR TRADITION – תּוֹרָה

The word תּוֹרָה means "teaching" and is the name of the Five Books of Moses. The תּוֹרָה teaches us how to live good and compassionate lives. The stories in the תּוֹרָה tell us about our ancestors Abraham and Sarah, Isaac and Rebecca, and Jacob, Leah, and Rachel. We read portions of the תּוֹרָה each week in the synagogue to help us remember its ideas and lessons.

Why do you think we reread the same words of the Torah year after year?

Why might it be helpful to read stories of our ancestors who lived thousands of years ago?

CONNECTIONS

Read the word in each column.

Connect each word in column א with a word in column בּ to make a phrase.

Say the phrase out loud.

א	בּ
שַׁבָּת	נִשְׁתַּנָּה
מַה	מִצְוָה
רֹאשׁ	שָׁלוֹם
יְצִיאַת	הַשָּׁנָה
בַּת	מִצְרַיִם

LESSON 15

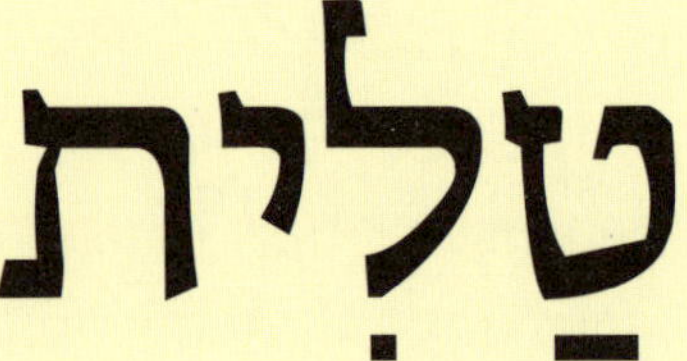

Tallit,
Prayer Shawl

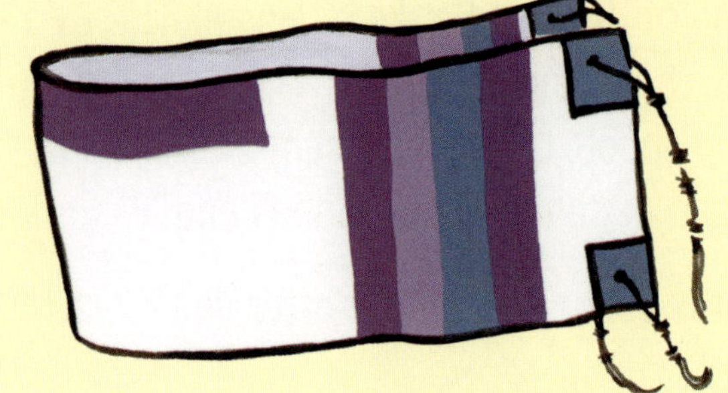

NEW LETTER

ט

LETTERS YOU KNOW. Say the name and sound of each letter.

בּ ת תּ שׁ מ ל כּ ה ר כ ב

ד א ו ק צ ע נ ן ח י ם

VOWELS YOU KNOW. Say the sound of each vowel.

ַ ָ ְ ֲ ִ ִי וֹ

ֹ

TET

1 טַ טְ טִ טוֹ טִי טֹ

2 טוֹ מוֹ טָ מָ טְ מְ

3 טָה טַשׁ בָּט עַט טָר נְטִי

SHAPE IT UP

What does ***Tet*** look like?

Close your eyes and picture the letter.

Draw it in the air or use your whole body to make the shape of the letter ***Tet***.

Make up a clue to remember ***Tet***.

READY, SET, READ

Read aloud all the words that begin with ***Tet***. Find all the words that end with ***Tet*** and read those too. Then read all the words that neither start nor end with ***Tet***.

1 טוֹן טִיב מָט אַט חַיָט מוֹטוֹ

2 טוֹב טַל אִטִי טָרִי שׁוֹט קָט

3 מִטָה מוֹט קָטָן חִטָה שָׁחַט לָטַשׁ

4 לְאַט מָטָר חָטָא מְעַט שְׁבָט בָּטַח

5 טַלִית טָהוֹר אָטָד טַעַם טִבְעִי טָמַן

6 קְטַנָה עֲטָרָה מִקְלָט חֲטָאִים הִבִּיטָה

7 שְׁבָטִים טוֹבִים בִּטָחוֹן נְטִילַת יָדַיִם

8 טַלִית שָׁנָה טוֹבָה יוֹם טוֹב

Great job!

I KNOW HEBREW!

Can you find these words above?

tallit, prayer shawl = טַלִית

holiday, festival = יוֹם טוֹב

Happy New Year = שָׁנָה טוֹבָה

On what Jewish holiday would you say שָׁנָה טוֹבָה?

Read and circle or highlight them.

SOUNDS LIKE

Read aloud each line.

Circle or highlight the Hebrew sounds on each line that are the same.

1	אַתָּה	הָאַתְּ	עַתָּה	כַּתִּיָה
2	מוֹתָה	טָאָר	תּוֹתָח	תֹּאַר
3	לָקַח	כַּלָּה	קַלָּה	כַּלַּת
4	מָכַר	כַּמָּה	חָמָת	מָחָר
5	וָנָע	עָנָו	בָּעָע	עָנָב
6	נָטַע	לְאַט	נָתָה	לְתָת
7	שְׁתִיָה	קְלִיטָה	כְּלִיתָ	שְׁלִיטָה
8	דַּקּוֹת	דַּכּוֹת	רַכָּת	כּוֹרָה

HEADS UP!

The letters תּ, ת, and ט make the same sound. What sound do they make?

WORD WIZARD

A phrase you know is hidden below! Cross out the Hebrew letters and their vowels that match the English sounds below. Write the remaining Hebrew letters with their vowels.

1	CHAH	3	MOH	5	N
2	YEE	4	LAH	6	EE

עִי שָׁ יִי נָ לָ ה

מוֹ טוֹ בָ כָ ה ן

What does the phrase mean? ____________

WRITING PRACTICE

ט

Write the Hebrew word for ***tallit, prayer shawl***.

טַלִית

Write the Hebrew words for ***Happy New Year***.

שָׁנָה טוֹבָה

Write the Hebrew words for ***holiday, festival***.

יוֹם טוֹב

I SPY

Find the Hebrew that sounds the same as the English in the box. Write the two Hebrew sounds on the line or read them to a partner.

1	HA	חֲ	חָ	הַ	תָ	הֱ	הַ הֱ
2	EE	אִי	צִ	אֲ	עִי	צִי	
3	NO	ווֹ	נוֹ	וֹ	כֹ	נֹ	
4	CHAH	ח	חֱ	הֱ	כַ	תַ	
5	VEE	וִי	יִ	יִי	וִיא	יֹ	
6	TAH	טַ	אֱ	מַ	תָּ	טְ	
7	N	ו	ר	ן	ד	נ	
8	VO	רוֹ	כֹ	בֹ	יֹ	ווֹ	
9	KEE	קִי	בִּי	לִ	כִּי	חִי	
10	M	ן	ם	ה	מ	ח	
11	TSAH	עַ	צָ	צְ	עֱ	צַ	
12	RO	רוֹ	דוֹ	תֹ	רֹ	וֹ	

OUR TRADITION – טַלִּית

טַלִּית is the Hebrew word for "prayer shawl." Many Jewish adults wear a טַלִּית during morning prayer services. The four corners of the טַלִּית have knotted fringes called צִיצִית. The תּוֹרָה tells us to look at the צִיצִית so that we will remember to follow God's commandments.

You might choose to wear a טַלִּית when you are a Jewish adult.

Draw a picture of yourself wearing a טַלִּית. Or, draw a picture of an adult you know wearing a טַלִּית.

SHOW WHAT YOU KNOW

Connect each Hebrew word with its English meaning.

BLESSING	צְדָקָה
PRAYER SHAWL	שַׁבָּת
JUSTICE	בְּרָכָה
SHABBAT	טַלִּית

TORAH	הַבְדָּלָה
GOING UP	בַּת
SEPARATION	תּוֹרָה
DAUGHTER	עֲלִיָּה

HOLY	שְׁמַע
TO LIFE	וְאָהַבְתָּ
HEAR	לְחַיִּים
AND YOU SHALL LOVE	קָדוֹשׁ

PROPHET	מִצְוָה
BRAIDED BREAD	שַׁמָּשׁ
HELPER	נָבִיא
COMMANDMENT	חַלָּה

CHECKPOINT CHALLENGE

Show off your Hebrew reading skills!

Read aloud each word. Give yourself one point for every word read correctly.

1	אוֹת	2	רִבּוֹנוֹ	3	כְּבוֹד	4	קָדוֹשׁ
5	טָהוֹר	6	מִצְווֹת	7	חוֹל	8	טוֹב
9	צִיּוֹן	10	כֹּהֲנִים	11	נָכוֹן	12	שָׁלוֹם
13	הַמּוֹצִיא	14	נוֹרָא	15	עוֹלָם	16	צוֹם
17	קוֹל	18	רֹאשׁ	19	לָשׁוֹן	20	תּוֹרָה

Earn another point for each word you can translate into English.

How did you do?

LESSON 16

אֱמֶת

Truth

LETTERS YOU KNOW. Say the name and sound of each letter.

בּ ת תּ שׁ מ ל כּ ה ר כ ב

ד א ו ק צ ע נ ן ח י ם

ט

VOWELS YOU KNOW. Say the sound of each vowel.

◌ַ ◌ָ ◌ְ ◌ֲ ◌ִ ◌ִי ◌וֹ

◌ֹ

NEW VOWELS

◌ֶ ◌ֱ

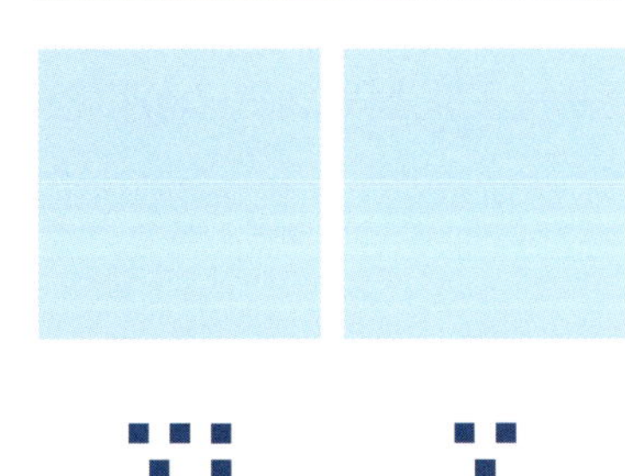

1	דֶ	בֶּ	תֶ	טֶ	אֱ	יֶ
2	שֶׁ	עֱ	מֶ	לֶ	קֶ	צֶ
3	תֶּם	עֶד	רֶב	חֱלִי	דֶשׁ	יֶה

SHAPE IT UP

What does ◌ֶ sound like? Make a hand motion to show the shape of ◌ֶ as you say its sound.

What does ◌ֱ sound like? Make a hand motion to show the shape of ◌ֱ as you say its sound.

READY, SET, READ

Choose two lines for a partner to read aloud. Then have your partner choose two lines for you to read. Continue until you've each read every line on the page.

1 אֶת אֶל שֶׁלִי שֶׁלֹא אֱמֶת אַתֶּן

2 אֲשֶׁר שֶׁמֶשׁ יֶלֶד לָכֶם אֹהֶל אֶבֶן

3 אַתֶּם נֶצַח חֹדֶשׁ כֹּתֶל טֶרֶם אֶחָד

4 רוֹצֶה שֶׁבַע עֶרֶב מוֹרֶה נֶאֱמָן שְׁמוֹנֶה

5 וְנֶאֱמַר מְחַיֶּה רוֹעֶה עוֹלֶה הֶחֱלִיט יִהְיֶה

6 לְעוֹלָם וָעֶד תּוֹרַת אֱמֶת מִצְוָה אֶתְכֶם

7 אֲרוֹן הַקֹּדֶשׁ כֶּתֶר תּוֹרָה וַיֹּאמֶר אֱלֹהִים

8 אֱלֹהִים הַמּוֹצִיא לֶחֶם אֱמֶת וְצֶדֶק

I KNOW HEBREW!

Can you find these Hebrew words above?

truth = אֱמֶת

God = אֱלֹהִים

Who brings forth bread = הַמּוֹצִיא לֶחֶם

the Holy Ark = אֲרוֹן הַקֹּדֶשׁ

Read and circle or highlight them.

EXTRA CREDIT

What is the first letter in the Hebrew word for truth? ___

How many other words above start with that letter? ___

PRAYER PRACTICE

All the words to the right are found in prayers or blessings. Practice reading them aloud.

The word לֶחֶם means bread. We say a blessing over bread on Shabbat. What is the name of the braided bread we eat on Shabbat? Write it here:

____

The word אֶחָד means one. We say an important prayer about our belief in one God. Can you remember the name of that prayer?

(Hint: the name of the prayer starts with a ***Shin***.)

Write its name in Hebrew here:________________

1 הַמוֹצִיא לֶחֶם

2 וַיֹאמֶר מֹשֶׁה

3 לְעוֹלָם וָעֶד

4 אֲדֹנָי אֶחָד

5 מִי כָמֹכָה נֶאְדָר בַּקֹדֶשׁ

6 אֱלֹהִים בָּרָא אֵת הַשָׁמַיִם

7 אֲשֶׁר אָנֹכִי מְצַוֶה אֶתְכֶם

8 כִּי עֶבֶד נֶאֱמָן קָרָאתָ לוֹ

HEADS UP!

Sometimes, the dot on the letter שׁ has to do two jobs. You can call it the double-duty dot.

מֹשֶׁה = מֹ שֶׁה

Can you explain what two jobs the dot has to do in these words?

מֹשֶׁה   עֹשֶׂר   שָׁלֹשׁ   רֹשֶׁם   קֹדֶשׁ

I SPY

Find the Hebrew word on each line that sounds the same as the English in the box.
Write the Hebrew word on the line or read it to a partner.

#	English				Write
1	ALIYAH	צִיּוֹן	עֲלִיָּה	הֲלָכָה	עֲלִיָּה
2	TALLIT	מִנְיָן	טוֹבָה	טַלִּית	
3	SHALOM	עוֹלָם	אָרוֹן	שָׁלוֹם	
4	MATZAH	הַמּוֹצִיא	מַצָּה	מִנְחָה	
5	AMIDAH	תְּקִיעָה	נְשָׁמָה	עֲמִידָה	
6	KADDISH	צַדִּיק	קַדִּישׁ	בְּרִית	
7	SHEMA	שְׁמַע	שַׁמָּשׁ	שַׁבָּת	

Describe what שָׁלוֹם means to you.

WRITING PRACTICE

Write the Hebrew word for ***truth***.

אֱמֶת

Write the Hebrew word for ***God***.

אֱלֹהִים

Write the Hebrew words for the ***Holy Ark***.

אֲרוֹן הַקֹּדֶשׁ

Write the Hebrew words for ***Who brings forth bread***.

הַמּוֹצִיא לֶחֶם

OUR TRADITION – אֱמֶת

The Hebrew word אֱמֶת means "truth."

In our prayers we say that God's words are true and righteous: אֱמֶת וְצֶדֶק.

The Ten Commandments instruct us to tell the truth—אֱמֶת.

Relationships between people must be built on אֱמֶת, on trust and truth.

Why is it important to tell the truth—אֱמֶת—to our family and friends?

SHOW WHO YOU KNOW

Match each Hebrew name with its translation. Read each match aloud.
Do you know anyone with those names?

MIRIAM	חַנָּה
REBECCA	דְּבוֹרָה
HANNAH	רִבְקָה
DEBORAH	מִרְיָם

MOSES	אָדָם
BENJAMIN	מֹשֶׁה
ADAM	דָּוִד
DAVID	בִּנְיָמִן

Passover
the feast of unleavened bread

LETTERS YOU KNOW. Say the name and sound of each letter.

בּ ת תּ שׁ מ ל כּ ה ר כ ב

ד א ו ק צ ע נ ן ח י ם

ט

VOWELS YOU KNOW. Say the sound of each vowel.

ַ ָ ְ ֲ ִ ִי וֹ

ֹ ֶ ֱ

NEW LETTER

PAY

1 פּוֹ פֶּ פַּ פְּ פֹּ פָּ

2 פֶּה פְּרִי פֹּה פֶּן פַּת פֶּתִי

3 פְּשָׁ פֶּשַׁ צִפּוֹ כַּפִּי טִפָּ פֶּרֶך

Which word above sounds like something you write with? Write it in Hebrew here:____________

SHAPE IT UP

What does ***Pay*** look like? Close your eyes and picture the letter.
Draw it in the air or use your whole body to make the shape of the letter ***Pay***.

Make up a clue to remember ***Pay***.

READY, SET, READ

Remember that the letter ***Pay*** makes the sound of the English letter ***P***.
Read aloud lines 1-3 like you're **p**owerful. Read lines 4-6 in a **p**olite voice.
Read lines 7-8 with a **p**ause between each sound.

1 אַפּוֹ פִּיל פָּנָה פַּחַד מִפִּי פֶּרַח

2 טִפָּה כַּפַּיִם צִפּוֹר פְּתַח דַּפִּים כַּפִּית

3 פְּשָׁט פַּעַם פֶּלֶא פֶּשַׁע פֶּרֶק כִּפָּה

4 פּוֹדֶה מַפָּה פָּקַד פָּחוֹת יִפֹּל תִּפֹּל

5 פִּדְיוֹן פַּרְצִי פְּלוֹנִי יִשְׁפֹּט מִשְׁפָּט פַּרְעֹה

6 פָּרָשָׁה כַּפָּרָה מַשְׁפִּיעַ צִפּוֹרָה עִפָּרוֹן

7 פְּעָמִים פָּתַחְתָּ אַלְפַּיִם הַשְׁפָּעָה פִּתְאֹם

8 מִשְׁפָּחָה מִשְׁפָּטִים מִתְפַּלְלִים פְּרָחִים

Great job!

Now read any four words **p**erfectly. Give yourself a **p**at on the back!

I KNOW HEBREW!

Can you find these Hebrew words above?

family = מִשְׁפָּחָה

kippah, skullcap = כִּפָּה

pencil = עִפָּרוֹן

Read and circle or highlight them.

EXTRA CREDIT

Can you find the Hebrew word for ***Pharaoh*** in the lines above? (Hint: it's on line 5.)

What do you know about ***Pharaoh***?

RHYME TIME

Read aloud the words to the right. Find the two rhyming words on each line. Circle them or read them to a partner.

1	נוֹרָא	צוֹם	תּוֹרָה	אוֹת
2	יוֹרָם	מוֹצִיא	הוֹצִיא	הוֹלְכִים
3	תֶּרֶק	לֶחֶם	כֶּתֶר	רֶחֶם
4	פֶּרֶק	טִפָּה	פֶּרַח	כִּפָּה
5	טָהוֹר	טַלִּית	מִטָּה	שָׁחוֹר
6	פִּדְיוֹן	פְּעָמִים	פִּתְאֹם	עִפָּרוֹן

1	סַ	סִ	סִי	סוֹ	סֹ	סֶ
2	סַל	סַע	סֶלָה	סָב	סַם	סִיר
3	חַסְ	יְסוֹ	סִיָן	סַבְ	מִסְ	נַסֶ

SHAPE IT UP

What does ***Samech*** look like?

Close your eyes and picture the letter.

Draw it in the air or use your whole body to make the shape of the letter ***Samech***.

Make up a clue to remember ***Samech***.

READY, SET, READ

Read aloud the first word on every line. Next, read the second word on every line. Then take a minute to stretch or walk around the room. Now you're ready to read more! Practice reading aloud the words you haven't read yet.

1 כּוֹס סֶלַע מַס פֶּסַח סְתָו סִיוָן

2 סְתָם חֶסֶד סַבָּא סָבְתָּא חֲסִיד כַּסְפּוֹ

3 נִיסָן סִדְרָה חַסְדוֹ סַנְדָּק יְסוֹד מִסְפָּר

4 מָסֹרֶת נִסִים נִכְנָס כְּסוֹד מְנַסֶה לַעֲסֹק

5 סְבִיבוֹן מִסָבִיב בָּסִיס הִסְפִּיד וְנִסְכּוֹ מַחְסִי

6 מְסַפֶּרֶת כְּנֶסֶת נִסְפָּח הַכְנָסַת מַסְפִּיק

7 חֲסָדִים חֲסִידִים פַּרְנָסָה סְלִיחָה סְלִיחוֹת

8 פֶּסַח כַּרְפַּס חֲרוֹסֶת מַצָה מָרוֹר פֶּסַח

Were any words especially challenging to read? Practice reading those again.

HOLIDAY CHALLENGE

Read all the words on line 8 above. All the words on line 8 are from a holiday. Write the name of that holiday in English here:

____

How many of those are words for things you can eat?

____

WRITING PRACTICE

פ

ס

Write the Hebrew word for ***Passover***.

פֶּסַח

Write the Hebrew word for ***kindness***.

חֶסֶד

Write the Hebrew word for ***kippah, skullcap***.

כִּפָּה

Write the Hebrew word for ***family***.

מִשְׁפָּחָה

WORD BUBBLES

With your eyes shut, point to a spot on the page. Read the word closest to where your finger lands.

Add the number in the circle to your score. Do it three times and see how high you can score. Play with a partner and see who scores higher.

Want a higher score? Earn one point for each word translated correctly.

OUR TRADITION – פֶּסַח

When our people were slaves in Egypt, God sent מֹשֶׁה to lead us out of Egypt to freedom. We celebrate this event each spring with the festival of פֶּסַח. Every year we retell the פֶּסַח story when we read the haggadah.

Draw a picture or write about how you celebrate the festival of פֶּסַח. What is your favorite part of פֶּסַח?

THE פֶּסַח SEDER

Read aloud each Hebrew word and its English meaning. Read each sentence describing a פֶּסַח food. What is the correct Hebrew word to each question?

מָרוֹר	מַצָּה	חֲרוֹסֶת	כַּרְפַּס	יַיִן
bitter herbs	matzah	chopped apples and nuts, *charoset*	greens	wine

1 Everyone was in a hurry to leave Egypt and did not have time to wait for the bread dough to rise. My dough hardened into a flat, crunchy kind of bread.

Who am I? ____________________

2 I am the greens on the seder plate. I represent springtime and new life. I am dipped into salt water to remind us of the tears we cried when we were slaves.

Who am I? ____________________

3 I taste bitter. I am a reminder of our bitter lives as slaves.

Who am I? ____________________

4 I remind everyone of the bricks we had to make when we were slaves in Egypt.

Who am I? ____________________

5 I am a sweet liquid. I am poured into a glass four times during the seder. Each time reminds us of God's four promises to bring us from slavery to freedom.

Who am I? ____________________

LESSON 18

שׁוֹפָר

Shofar

LETTERS YOU KNOW. Say the name and sound of each letter.

בּ ת תּ שׁ מ ל כּ ה ר כ ב

ד א ו ק צ ע נ ן ח י ם

ט פּ ס

VOWELS YOU KNOW. Say the sound of each vowel.

◌ַ ◌ָ ◌ְ ◌ֲ ◌ִ ◌ִי ◌וֹ

◌ֹ ◌ֶ ◌ֱ

NEW LETTER

פ

FAY

1	פִי	פֶ	פַ	פוֹ	פְ	פֹ
2	פֶ	פֶּ	פ	פּ	פֹ	פֹּ
3	נָפַ	אֹפֶ	שֶׁפַ	לִפְ	תְּפִ	צוֹפִ

SHAPE IT UP

What does *Fay* look like?
Close your eyes and picture the letter.
Draw it in the air or use your whole body to make the shape of the letter *Fay*.

Make up a clue to remember *Fay*

____________________.

HEADS UP!

The letters פּ and פ make different sounds.

What sound does פּ make?
What sound does פ make?
How do they look different?

Make up a clue to help you remember the difference between פּ and פ.

____

READY, SET, READ

Read lines 1-4 in a soft voice. Read lines 5-8 in a regular voice.

1 יָפֶה עָפָר כְּפִי נֶפֶשׁ חֹפֶשׁ צוֹפֶה

2 אֹפִי תָּפַס נָפַל אָפָה יָפִים נַפְשִׁי

3 אֹפֶן אֶפֶס צָפוֹן שֶׁפַע כֹּפֶר יִפְתֶּה

4 אָסַפְתָּ אֶפְשָׁר תְּפִלָּה מַפְטִיר תִּפְתַּח לִפְעָמִים

5 תְּפִלּוֹת סְפָרִים סוֹפְרִים לְפָנִים צוֹפִיָּה אַפְקִיד

6 לִפְדוֹת נוֹפְלִים טוֹטָפֹת נַפְשְׁכֶם תִּפְאֶרֶת

7 אֲפִיקוֹמָן הַפְטָרָה שׁוֹפְטִים כְּמִפְעָלוֹ תְּפִילִין

8 שׁוֹפָר תְּפִלָּה תְּפִילִין מַפְטִיר הַפְטָרָה

I KNOW HEBREW!

Can you find these Hebrew words above?

prayer = תְּפִלָּה

Haftarah = הַפְטָרָה

shofar = שׁוֹפָר

soul = נֶפֶשׁ

afikoman = אֲפִיקוֹמָן

Read and circle or highlight them.

STRIKE A POSE

Show off your best שׁוֹפָר blowing stance!

Make the sound of a שׁוֹפָר too (if it's OK with everyone else in the room).

WRITING PRACTICE

פ פ פ

Write the Hebrew word for ***shofar***.

שׁוֹפָר שׁוֹפָר

Write the Hebrew word for ***soul***.

נֶפֶשׁ נֶפֶשׁ

Write the Hebrew word for ***prayer***.

תְּפִלָּה תְּפִלָּה

Write the Hebrew word for ***afikoman***.

אֲפִיקוֹמָן אֲפִיקוֹמָן

Write the Hebrew word for ***Haftarah***.

הַפְטָרָה הַפְטָרָה

PRAYER PRACTICE

Find the Hebrew letters on each line that sound the same as the English in the box. Write the letters on the line or say them. Remember that some Hebrew letters sound alike.

1	D	תָּמִיד מְסַפְּרִים כְּבוֹד אֱלֹהִים
2	M	אֲשֶׁר אָנֹכִי מְצַוֶּה אֶתְכֶם הַיּוֹם
3	V	עַל לְבַבְכֶם וְעַל נַפְשְׁכֶם
4	F	נַפְשִׁי תִדּוֹם וְנַפְשִׁי כֶּעָפָר לַכֹּל תִּהְיֶה
5	T	קְשַׁרְתֶּם אֹתָם לְאוֹת עַל יֶדְכֶם
6	P	פּוֹתְחִים אֶת פִּיהֶם בְּשִׁירָה

OUR TRADITION — שׁוֹפָר

The שׁוֹפָר is made from a ram's horn. When it is blown, it makes a loud trumpeting sound.
In ancient times the שׁוֹפָר was blown to announce the beginning of Shabbat.
We blow the שׁוֹפָר on Rosh Hashanah and at the end of Yom Kippur.
On Rosh Hashanah the shofar is blown 100 times!

What do you think about or feel when you hear the sound of the שׁוֹפָר?

PICTURE PERFECT

Read each word aloud. Match the correct word with its picture.

טַלִּית

תּוֹרָה

שׁוֹפָר

פֶּסַח

אֲרוֹן הַקֹּדֶשׁ

CHECKPOINT CHALLENGE

Show off your Hebrew reading skills!

Read aloud each word. Give yourself one point for every word read correctly.

1	אֱלֹהִים	2	בֶּאֱמֶת	3	עֶבֶד	4	דֶלֶת
5	הֶבֶל	6	מְצַוֶה	7	חֶסֶד	8	טֶרֶם
9	יִהְיֶה	10	כֶּתֶר	11	תֹּכֶן	12	לֶחֶם
13	עֹמֶר	14	נֶאֱמָן	15	סֶלַע	16	עֶרֶב
17	פֶּסַח	18	נֶפֶשׁ	19	צֶדֶק	20	קֶרֶן
21	פֶּרֶק	22	אֲשֶׁר	23	כֹּתֶל	24	תֶּבֶן

Earn another point for each word you can translate into English.

How did you do?

עֵץ חַיִּים

Tree of Life

LETTERS YOU KNOW. Say the name and sound of each letter.

בּ ת תּ שׁ מ ל כּ ה ר כ ב

ד א ו ק צ ע נ ן ח י ם

ט פּ ס פ

VOWELS YOU KNOW. Say the sound of each vowel.

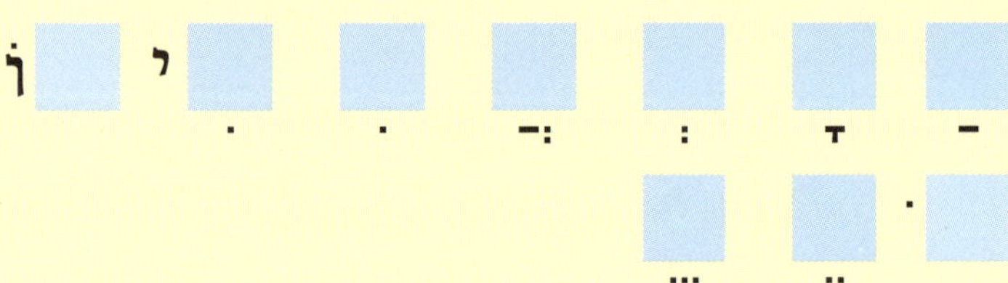

NEW LETTER

NEW VOWELS

1 שֵׁי פֵּי מֵי לֵי דֵ נֵי

2 פֵי סֵ טֵי יֵי עֵי כֵּ

3 סֵפֶּ כֹּהֵ אוֹמֵ הֵיטֵ דְרֵי שְׁרֵי

Read the lines above. Which Hebrew sound reminds you of a horse?

Write it in Hebrew here:______________

SHAPE IT UP

What does ֵ sound like?

Make a hand motion to show the shape of ֵ as you say its sound.

What does ֵי sound like?

Make a hand motion to show the shape of ֵי as you say its sound.

READY, SET, READ

Read aloud the lines below as if you were telling a story. Read lines 1-2 in a sad voice. Read lines 3-4 in a happy voice. The scary part is on lines 5-6, and the exciting part is on line 7. Line 8 is the last line of your "story." How will it end? You decide.

1 בֵּן שֵׁם יֵשׁ אֵלִי כֵּן אֵם

2 אֵין בֵּית נֵס בֵּין לֵב נֵר

3 חֵטְא אָמֵן סֵדֶר כָּשֵׁר סֵפֶר שְׁתֵּי

4 חָבֵר אוֹמֵר כֹּהֵן הַלֵּל דִּבֵּר עֵדֶן

5 לִבְנֵי תּוֹקֵעַ הֵיטֵב סוֹפֵר רוֹפֵא יוֹצֵר

6 אֱלֹהֵי פִּרְקֵי נִדְרֵי אַחֲרֵי חַסְדֵי תִּשְׁרֵי

7 אָמֵן לֵישֵׁב בְּצֵאת אוֹהֵב מְקַדֵּשׁ מַלְאֲכֵי

8 בְּרֵאשִׁית סֵפֶר תּוֹרָה נֵר תָּמִיד שָׁלוֹם עֲלֵיכֶם

I KNOW HEBREW!

Can you find the Hebrew words above?

Torah scroll, Five Books of Moses = סֵפֶר תּוֹרָה

seder = סֵדֶר

Eternal Light = נֵר תָּמִיד

amen = אָמֵן

heart = לֵב

Read and circle or highlight them. Find the Hebrew word we say at the end of a prayer or blessing.

Which line is it on?__________

(Hint: It means "so be it." When you say this word, you are saying you agree with the prayer or blessing.)

RHYME TIME

Read aloud the words to the right. Circle or highlight the two on each line that rhyme. Sing the rhyming words aloud.

1 בֶּן נֵר תֵּל כֵּן

2 אָמַר אָמֵן שָׁמֵן עֹמֶר

3 קוֹרֵא תּוֹקֵעַ שׁוֹמֵר שׁוֹמֵעַ

4 מִנְיָן מִקְוָה בִּנְיָן בָּנִים

5 טַהֵר טוֹבָה מַהֵר מִצְוָה

6 תִּפְאֶרֶת שַׁחֲרִית אוֹמְרוֹת סוֹפֶרֶת

7 צְדָקָה רַחֲמִים רַחֲמָן צַדִּיקִים

8 מַלְאֲכֵי פְּעָמִים פַּעֲמוֹן פִּרְקֵי

FINAL TZADEE

ץ

1 עֵץ קֵץ חֵץ רָץ אָץ נֵץ

2 עֵץ עֵצִים רָץ רָצָה לֵץ לֵיצָן

3 צֵץ צַע רֶץ פִּיץ רֶן צָה

SHAPE IT UP

What does ***Final Tzadee*** look like?
Close your eyes and picture the letter.
Draw it in the air or use your whole body to make the shape of the letter ***Final Tzadee***.

Make up a clue to remember ***Final Tzadee***.

HEADS UP!

There are five letters in the Hebrew alphabet that have a different form when they come at the end of a word.

When a צ comes at the end of a word, it is a ***Final*** ץ.

Can you name two other letters that have a final form?

READY, SET, READ

Read aloud the lines below. Then read again only the words that end with a ***Final Tzadee***.

1 אֶרֶץ חָמֵץ מַצָּה חָפֵץ קַיִץ אֹמֶץ

2 קוֹץ קוֹצִים בּוֹץ פָּרַץ קוֹפֵץ קוֹפֶצֶת

3 נוֹצֵץ לוֹחֵץ צַנְחָן עָצִיץ מִיץ נִמְצַץ

4 אִמֵץ אֶמְצַע מֶרֶץ אָמִיץ הֵצִיץ צַיִן

5 לִקְפֹּץ קְפִיצָה קָמָץ חוֹלֵץ חוֹלֵם הֵפִיץ

6 רוֹחֵץ רָחֲצָה יוֹעֵץ צִפֹּרֶן וְאֶמַץ פֶּרֶץ

7 לְשַׁבֵּץ נִצְטַוָּה מֵלִיץ צְבָעִים צָפוֹן חָמִיץ

8 עֵץ חַיִּים הַמּוֹצִיא לֶחֶם מִן הָאָרֶץ

I KNOW HEBREW!

Can you find these Hebrew words above?

Tree of Life = עֵץ חַיִּים

leavened food = חָמֵץ

Read and circle or highlight them.

Can you find the Hebrew word for the special food we eat during פֶּסַח?

Write it here. ______________________.

Does that word contain a ***Tzadee*** or a ***Final Tzadee***?

WRITING PRACTICE

צ

Write the Hebrew words for ***Tree of Life***.

עֵץ חַיִּים

Write the Hebrew word for ***leavened food***.

חָמֵץ

Write the Hebrew words for ***Torah scroll***.

סֵפֶר תּוֹרָה

Write the Hebrew words for ***Eternal Light***.

נֵר תָּמִיד

Write the Hebrew word for ***seder***.

סֵדֶר

Write the Hebrew word for ***amen***.

אָמֵן

ADD A TZADEE

Complete each word below by adding the correct form of the letter ***Tzadee***.
Then read all the words. When you read a word that contains a ***Tzadee***, stand up. When you read a word that contains a ***Final Tzadee***, sit down.

1 עֵ__ 2 מַ__ָה 3 מִ__ְוָה

4 הָאָרֶ__ 5 חָמֵ__ 6 __ְדָקָה

7 __ְבָעִים 8 __ִוָּה 9 קוֹפֵ__

10 הַמּוֹ__ִיא 11 קָמַ__ 12 __ַדִּיק

OUR TRADITION – עֵץ חַיִּים

A ***Tree of Life***–עֵץ חַיִּים–is one of the symbols of the Torah.

In fact, the two wooden rollers around which the תּוֹרָה scroll is wrapped are called עֲצֵי חַיִּים–trees of life. The תּוֹרָה is like a tree because just as a tree is strong and offers food, so, too, the Torah gives the Jewish people strength and nourishes our souls.

How can the Torah give the Jewish people strength and nourishment? Talk about it with a partner.

CONNECTIONS

Connect the beginning of a phrase with its ending. Say the phrase out loud.

1	הַמּוֹצִיא	נִשְׁתַּנָּה
2	מַה	תּוֹרָה
3	עֵץ	מִצְרַיִם
4	סֵפֶר	לֶחֶם
5	יְצִיאַת	חַיִּים

6	יוֹם	עֲלֵיכֶם
7	אֲרוֹן	טוֹבָה
8	נֵר	הַקֹּדֶשׁ
9	שָׁנָה	תָּמִיד
10	שָׁלוֹם	טוֹב

ALEF BET CHART

You have learned 5 new letters in Lessons 15-19:

ט פּ ס פ ץ

Turn to the ***Alef Bet*** chart on page 160. Color in the new letters.

Can you say the name and sound of each letter you now know?

LESSON 20

יִשְׂרָאֵל

Israel

NEW LETTER

שׂ

LETTERS YOU KNOW. Say the name and sound of each letter.

בּ ת תּ שׁ מ ל כּ ה ר כ ב

ד א ו ק צ ע נ ן ח י ם

ט פּ ס פ ץ

VOWELS YOU KNOW. Say the sound of each vowel.

ַ ָ ְ ֲ ִ ִי וֹ

ֹ ֶ ֱ ֵ ֵי

SIN

שׂ

1	שָׂ	שִׂי	שֵׂי	שׂוֹ	שֶׂ	שֵׂ
2	שֵׂ	שֵׂ	שִׂי	שֵׂי	שׂוֹ	שׂוֹ
3	מַשָׂ	שָׂשׂוֹ	שֶׂבַ	שָׂפָ	יִשָׂ	עֶשְׂ

SHAPE IT UP

What does ***Sin*** look like?

Close your eyes and picture the letter.

Draw it in the air or use your whole body to make the shape of the letter ***Sin***.

Make up a clue to remember ***Sin***.

HEADS UP!

The letters שׁ and שׂ make different sounds.

What sound does שׁ make?

What sound does שׂ make?

How do they look different?

Make up a clue to help you remember the difference between שׁ and שׂ.

READY, SET, READ

Read aloud all the words that start with ***Sin***. Next, read all the words that have a ***Sin*** in the middle of the word. Then, read all the words that do not have a ***Sin***.

1	שֶׂה	שִׂים	שַׂר	שָׂם	שַׂק	שִׂיא
2	שָׂדָה	שָׂנֵא	שָׂמַח	עֶשֶׂר	עֹשֶׂה	מַשָׂא
3	שָׂרָה	שָׂרָה	שָׂמָה	שָׂמָה	שַׂעַר	שָׂשׂוֹן
4	שֵׂעָר	שָׂכָר	שָׂפָה	יִשָׂא	בָּשָׂר	שֵׂכֶל
5	שָׂדֶה	פָּשַׂט	שֶׂבַע	עֶשֶׂר	עָשָׂה	תַּיִשׂ
6	שִׂמְחַת	תּוֹרָה	שְׁמוֹנֶה	עֶשְׂרֵה	עֲשֶׂרֶת	הַדִּבְּרוֹת
7	שְׁמַע	יִשְׂרָאֵל	שִׂים	שָׁלוֹם	עוֹשֶׂה	שָׁלוֹם
8	עַם	יִשְׂרָאֵל	בְּנֵי	יִשְׂרָאֵל	אֶרֶץ	יִשְׂרָאֵל

I KNOW HEBREW!

Can you find the Hebrew words above?

Ten Commandments = עֲשֶׂרֶת הַדִּבְּרוֹת

Rejoicing of the Torah = שִׂמְחַת תּוֹרָה

Israel = יִשְׂרָאֵל

WORD RIDDLE

I am a holiday we celebrate each year when we finish reading the entire תּוֹרָה.

We then begin reading the תּוֹרָה from the very first word all over again.

My name begins with שׂ. What holiday am I?

PRAYER PRACTICE

The phrases below are all from prayers you may find in a siddur, a prayer book. Practice reading them. Write or say the number of words that have a ***Sin*** in each line.

1 ____ שְׁמַע יִשְׂרָאֵל

2 ____ שִׂים שָׁלוֹם טוֹבָה...בְּרָכָה

3 ____ עוֹשֶׂה שָׁלוֹם...יַעֲשֶׂה שָׁלוֹם

4 ____ בּוֹרֵא מִינֵי בְשָׂמִים

5 ____ בְּלִי רֵאשִׁית בְּלִי תַכְלִית

6 ____ וְאֵין שֵׁנִי לְהַמְשִׁיל לוֹ

7 ____ לֹא תִשָּׂא אֶת שֵׁם (אֱלֹהִים)...לַשָּׁוְא

8 ____ וַיִּשְׁבֹּת בַּיּוֹם הַשְּׁבִיעִי...מְלַאכְתּוֹ אֲשֶׁר עָשָׂה

9 ____ לִשְׁמֹעַ לִלְמֹד...לְלַמֵּד לִשְׁמֹר וְלַעֲשׂוֹת

10 ____ בַּיּוֹם הַשְּׁבִיעִי שָׁבַת וַיִּנָּפַשׁ

WRITING PRACTICE

שׁ

Write the Hebrew word for ***Israel***.

יִשְׂרָאֵל

Write the Hebrew words for ***Rejoicing of the Torah***.

שִׂמְחַת תּוֹרָה

SOUNDS LIKE

Read aloud each line. Find the Hebrew sounds on each line that are the same. Circle, say, or write them.

#					
1	עֵד	אֵם	אֵד	צֵד	עֵד אֵד
2	כֹּס	שָׂם	בֹּס	סַם	
3	לֹא	עוֹל	לוֹ	צֹל	
4	יָכוֹל	קוֹל	כֹּל	כְּכֹל	
5	תֵּוָת	טֵבֵת	בֵּיתָה	תֵּוֵט	
6	עוֹשֶׂה	עֹשֶׂר	אֹסֶה	אֲשֶׁר	
7	כּוֹפֵר	קֹפֵר	בּוֹקֶר	בּוֹכֶה	
8	עֲשָׂרוֹת	עָשִׂיתִי	עֲרָסוֹת	אָסִיתִי	

HEADS UP!

The letters שׂ and ס make the same sound. What sound do they make?

OUR TRADITION — יִשְׂרָאֵל

Jewish people have lived in יִשְׂרָאֵל for more than 3,000 years.

It is the country where our ancestors Abraham and Sarah lived. It is the country where King David ruled. יִשְׂרָאֵל is the country where the modern state of Israel, our homeland, was reborn. יִשְׂרָאֵל has a special place in the hearts of Jews around the world.

Have you or anyone you know visited יִשְׂרָאֵל?

TOURING יִשְׂרָאֵל

Below are the names of eight places in יִשְׂרָאֵל.

Read aloud the Hebrew name of each place.

Then look at the map of יִשְׂרָאֵל.

Write or say the matching number for each English name.

1 צְפַת

2 תֵּל-אָבִיב

3 אֵילַת

4 הֶרְצְלִיָּה

5 מְצָדָה

6 חֵיפָה

7 יְרוּשָׁלַיִם

8 בְּאֵר שֶׁבַע

LESSON 21

חַג שָׂמֵחַ

Happy Holiday

LETTERS YOU KNOW. Say the name and sound of each letter.

בּ ת תּ שׁ מ ל כּ ה ר כ ב

ד א ו ק צ ע נ ן ח י ם

ט פּ ס פ ץ שׂ

VOWELS YOU KNOW. Say the sound of each vowel.

◌ַ ◌ָ ◌ְ ◌ֲ ◌ִ ◌ִי ◌וֹ

◌ֹ ◌ֶ ◌ֱ ◌ֵ ◌ֵי

NEW LETTER

ג

GIMMEL

1 גַ גוֹ גִי גֶ גַ גֵי

2 גַג גַלוֹ גַבֵּי גַנֵי גִיס גִיר

3 גֹדֶ גִבּוֹ גָאַ הָג גִטִי גוֹלָ

SHAPE IT UP

What does ***Gimmel*** look like?

Close your eyes and picture the letter.

Draw it in the air or use your whole body to make the shape of the letter ***Gimmel***.

Make up a clue to remember ***Gimmel***.

READY, SET, READ

Read aloud the lines below. Then give yourself a pat on the back. Choose a line to read again to a partner. Ask your partner to decide how to let you know if you did a good job. Then switch.

1 חַג גַן גְדִי גֵר דָג גַם

2 גֹלֶם גֹדֶל מָגֵן עֹנֶג גֶפֶן גִיל

3 גִבּוֹר גוֹלֵל גוֹמֵל גָאַל גֶשֶׁם דֶגֶל

4 גוֹלָה מְגִלָה הִשִׂיג מִנְהָג גָדוֹל גִטִים

5 אַגָדָה אֶתְרֹג רֶגֶל הִגְדִיל חַגִים גְדוֹלָה

6 גְמָרָא נָגִילָה הִגִיעַ חֲגִיגָה שִׁגָעוֹן פִּתְגָם

7 מָגֵן אַבְרָהָם מְגִלָה עֹנֶג שַׁבָּת יִתְגַדַל

8 הַגָדָה חַד גַדְיָא מָגֵן דָוִד מָגֵן אָבוֹת

I KNOW HEBREW!

Can you find these Hebrew words above?

scroll = מְגִלָה

haggadah = הַגָדָה

Shield of David, Jewish Star = מָגֵן דָוִד

Read and circle or highlight them.

EXTRA CREDIT

The Jewish star is known as the ***Magen David***—the Shield of David. David was an ancient king of Israel. We can see this symbol on the flag of Israel. Can you find the Hebrew words for ***Magen David*** above? Write the line number. ______

Do you know what the flag of Israel looks like? Look for it on page 119, then draw it below.

I SPY

Read each line.

Find the Hebrew letter that sounds the same as the English in the box. Circle it.

1	B	ג	בּ (circled)	כ	ב	פּ	כּ
2	T	ץ	ס	מ	ח	ט	ל
3	M	ט	כ	ת	ס	ח	ם
4	N	ר	ע	ן	ד	כ	ו
5	S	ה	שׁ	ט	שׂ	מ	ת
6	V	ו	נ	פ	ג	י	ן
7	Y	ן	א	ץ	י	ו	ע
8	G	ס	ו	ג	ל	ר	נ
9	TS	ץ	שׁ	א	ק	ע	ן
10	P	תּ	פּ	ב	כּ	פ	בּ

HEADS UP!

When חַ comes at the end of a word, we read the vowel first and then the letter. שָׁמֵחַ sounds like שָׁמֵאַח.

1	כֹּחַ	מֹחַ	רֵיחַ	נֹחַ	שִׁיחַ	אֹחַ
2	יָרֵחַ	בַּכֹּחַ	הַמֹחַ	לְנֹחַ	כְּשִׁיחַ	טִיחַ
3	רֵחַ	מִיחַ	שִׁיחַ	גִּיחַ	רֹחַ	נוֹחַ

READY, SET, READ

The first word on line 1, שָׂמֵחַ, means "happy." Read lines 1-4 in a happy voice. Read lines 5-8 in your regular voice, except when you come to the word שָׂמֵחַ. Read that word in a happy voice.

1 שָׂמֵחַ יָרֵחַ אוֹרֵחַ נָשִׂיחַ מֵנִיחַ בַּכֹּחַ

2 מָשִׁיחַ פּוֹקֵחַ סוֹלֵחַ פּוֹתֵחַ פָּתַח לִפְתֹּחַ

3 לְשַׁבֵּחַ מְנַצֵּחַ שׁוֹלֵחַ מָנוֹחַ שָׁלִיחַ מַפְתֵּחַ

4 מַצְמִיחַ מִשְׁלוֹחַ הִצְלִיחַ לוֹקֵחַ לְשַׂמֵּחַ פּוֹרֵחַ

5 מַשְׁגִּיחַ הַשְׁגָּחָה אָשִׂיחַ שִׂיחָה מְשַׂמֵּחַ שָׂמַח

6 הִבְטִיחַ בָּטַח טוֹרֵחַ טָרַח פִּקֵּחַ נִפְקַח

7 בּוֹרֵחַ לִבְרֹחַ בָּרַח לִסְלֹחַ סָלַח סְלִיחָה

8 מָשִׁיחַ חַג שָׂמֵחַ פֶּסַח הַגָּדָה מְגִלָּה

I KNOW HEBREW!

Can you find the Hebrew words above?

happy holiday = חַג שָׂמֵחַ

moon = יָרֵחַ

Read and circle or highlight them.

PRAYER PRACTICE

The phrases below are all from prayers you may find in a siddur, a prayer book. Practice reading them aloud. Put a check next to the two lines you find most challenging.

1 ______ לְשַׁבֵּחַ לַאֲדוֹן הַכֹּל

2 ______ הָאֵל הַגָּדוֹל הַגִּבּוֹר וְהַנּוֹרָא

3 ______ לְעֵת תָּכִין מַטְבֵּחַ

4 ______ לְהוֹדוֹת לְהַלֵּל לְשַׁבֵּחַ

5 ______ שְׂמֵחִים בְּצֵאתָם וְשָׂשִׂים בְּבֹאָם

6 ______ מְשַׂמֵּחַ צִיּוֹן בְּבָנֶיהָ

SAY A BLESSING

Practice reading these endings to five different blessings, בְּרָכוֹת.

When do we recite each one? Write it on the blank lines.

1 בּוֹרֵא פְּרִי הַגָּפֶן ______

2 בּוֹרֵא פְּרִי הָעֵץ ______

3 בּוֹרֵא פְּרִי הָאֲדָמָה ______

4 בּוֹרֵא מְאוֹרֵי הָאֵשׁ ______

5 בּוֹרֵא מִינֵי בְשָׂמִים ______

THE ADDED DOT

Add a dot to one member of each set of family letters. Then say or write the sound of each letter.

ב ב   כ כ   פ פ   ת ת

B ___   ___ ___   ___ ___   ___ ___

Which letter did not change its sound when you added a dot?

RHYME TIME

Read the Hebrew words below. Connect the rhyming words, then sing them out loud.

1	רֶגֶל	הַגָּדָה
2	מָשִׁיחַ	סוֹלֵחַ
3	אַגָּדָה	דֶּגֶל
4	פּוֹקֵחַ	שָׁלִיחַ
5	כֹּחַ	גּוֹמֵל
6	יָרֵחַ	טָהוֹר
7	גּוֹלֵל	שָׂמֵחַ
8	גִּבּוֹר	מֹחַ

WRITING PRACTICE

ג

Write the Hebrew words for ***happy holiday***.

חַג שָׂמֵחַ

Write the Hebrew word for ***haggadah***.

הַגָּדָה

Write the Hebrew word for ***scroll***.

מְגִלָּה

Write the Hebrew words for ***Shield of David***.

מָגֵן דָּוִד

OUR TRADITION – חַג שָׂמֵחַ

The word חַג means "holiday" or "festival." The word שָׂמֵחַ means "happy" or "joyous."

When we say חַג שָׂמֵחַ, we wish someone a happy holiday.

Name a holiday when you might say חַג שָׂמֵחַ.

WORD WIZARD

Follow the directions to discover a hidden phrase.

Cross out the Hebrew letters and their vowels that match the English sounds.

Write the remaining Hebrew letters and their vowels.

1

1 SAY	4 M	7 SHOH
2 TEH	5 PEH	8 GEH
3 NEE	6 VEE	9 HAH

סֵיחַטֶנִיגם   פֶּשָׂוִימֵשׁוֹגֶחַהַ

_____ _____   _____ _____ _____

_____ _____   _____ _____ _____

What does it mean? ______________________

When do we use it? ______________________

2

1 YAH	4 SAH	7 KAH
2 FOH	5 N	8 EH
3 CHAH	6 GEE	9 DAY

יַפוֹשַׁחַבַּשָׁתן   גִיקַשָׁעֱלוֹדֵים

_____ _____ _____   _____ _____ _____ _____

_____ _____ _____   _____ _____ _____ _____

What does it mean? ______________________

When do we use it? ______________________

CHECKPOINT CHALLENGE

Play Tic-Tac-Toe with a partner. If you read the word correctly, mark the square with an X or an O.

חָבֵר	בֵּית-כְּנֶסֶת	אֵין
כֹּהֵן	קַדֵּשׁ	מָגֵן
טֵבֵת	חֵטְא	וֵאלֹהֵי

מַלְאֲכֵי	כֵּן	יֵצֶר
נֵרוֹת	מֵבִין	הַלֵּל
פֵּרוֹת	עֵדֶן	סֵפֶר

פִּרְקֵי	יוֹצֵר	סוֹפֵר
שֵׂכֶל	שֵׁם	בּוֹרֵא
שָׂמֵחַ	מֹשֶׁה	תֵּשַׁע

קִדּוּשׁ

NEW VOWEL

וּ ֻ

LETTERS YOU KNOW. Say the name and sound of each letter.

בּ ת תּ שׁ מ ל כּ ה ר כ ב

ד א ו ק צ ע נ ן ח י ם

ט פּ ס פ ץ שׂ ג

VOWELS YOU KNOW. Say the sound of each vowel.

ַ ָ ְ ֲ ִ ִי וֹ

ֹ ֶ ֱ ֵ ֵי

1	סוּ שׁוּ טוּ נוּ מוּ צוּ
2	בֻּ גֻ שֻׁ רֻ קֻ תֻּ
3	הוּא לָנוּ אָנוּ בָּנוּ צוּד כֻּלוֹ

SHAPE IT UP

What does וּ sound like?

Make a hand motion to show the shape of וּ as you say its sound.

What does ֻ sound like?

Make a hand motion to show the shape of ֻ as you say its sound.

What is the sound a cow makes? Write it in Hebrew here:________________

What sound is the opposite of "old"? Write it in Hebrew here:________________

READY, SET, READ

Read aloud the lines below. Point to your belly when you read an "oo" vowel sound.

1 חֻמָּשׁ לוּחַ כֻּלָּם וְהָיוּ סֻכָּה טֹבוּ

2 עָלֵינוּ לִבֵּנוּ סֻכּוֹת שָׁבוּעַ חֲנֻכָּה קִבּוּץ

3 קִדּוּשׁ שֻׁלְחָן מְשֻׁבָּח סִדּוּר מְצֻיָּן כֻּלָּנוּ

4 הַלְלוּיָה גְּדֻלָּה פָּסוּק יְשׁוּעָה נְטוּיָה אֲנַחְנוּ

5 וּבְנֻחֹה לוּלָב וְיָפֻצוּ וַיְכֻלּוּ וְיָנֻסוּ דַּיֵּנוּ

6 תְּמוּנָה וְצִוָּנוּ אֵלִיָּהוּ הַנָּבִיא בָּרְכוּ קֻשְׁיוֹת

7 קְדֻשָּׁה יְהוּדִים פּוּרִים יוֹם כִּפּוּר שָׁבוּעוֹת

8 יְרוּשָׁלַיִם אֱלֹהֵינוּ שֶׁהֶחֱיָנוּ אָבִינוּ מַלְכֵּנוּ

I KNOW HEBREW!

Can you find these Hebrew words above?

The Five Books of Moses = חֻמָּשׁ

Jerusalem = יְרוּשָׁלַיִם

Elijah the Prophet = אֵלִיָּהוּ הַנָּבִיא

Kiddush = קִדּוּשׁ

prayer book = סִדּוּר

Jews = יְהוּדִים

Read and circle or highlight them.

EXTRA CREDIT

Can you find the Hebrew word for ***prayer book*** in the lines above?

Write it here:

____

I SPY

Read aloud each line.

Find the Hebrew that sounds the same as the English in the box. Circle it or highlight it.

1	SHOO	שֻׁ	**שׁוּ**	שׁוֹ	שִׁי	שֶׁ	שֵׁי
2	FOH	פוּ	פָ	פוֹ	פִ	פְ	פֵי
3	AH	עֹ	עֱ	עִ	עֶ	עֲ	עוּ
4	SEE	שָׂ	שֶׂ	שׂוֹ	שֱׂ	שַׂ	שִׂי
5	YOH	יוּ	יֹ	יָ	יִי	יֵי	יֱ
6	PEH	פֱּ	פְּ	פַּ	פֶּ	פּוֹ	פֵּי
7	TSOO	צֵי	צְ	צוּ	צָ	צִ	צֹ
8	SOO	סַ	סוֹ	סֱ	סִי	סְ	סֵ
9	EH	אִי	אוּ	אָ	אֱ	אֶ	אֹ
10	TAY	טוֹ	טַ	טֱ	טֵי	טִ	טֹ

POWER READING

Practice reading these prayer phrases from the קִדּוּשׁ, which we recite over wine.

Write the number of words with the vowel וּ you find on each line.

1 ____ אֲשֶׁר קִדְּשָׁנוּ בְּמִצְווֹתָיו וְרָצָה בָנוּ

2 ____ וְשַׁבָּת...בְּאַהֲבָה וּבְרָצוֹן הִנְחִילָנוּ

3 ____ כִּי הוּא יוֹם תְּחִלָּה לְמִקְרָאֵי קֹדֶשׁ

4 ____ כִּי בָנוּ בָחַרְתָּ וְאוֹתָנוּ קִדַּשְׁתָּ

5 ____ בְּאַהֲבָה וּבְרָצוֹן הִנְחַלְתָּנוּ

6 ____ מְקַדֵּשׁ הַשַּׁבָּת

WRITING PRACTICE

Write the Hebrew words for ***the Five Books of Moses***.

חֻמָּשׁ

Write the Hebrew word for ***Jews***.

יְהוּדִים

Write the Hebrew word for ***Jerusalem***.

יְרוּשָׁלַיִם

Write the Hebrew word for ***prayer book***.

סִדּוּר

Write the Hebrew word for ***Kiddush***.

קִדּוּשׁ

Write the Hebrew words for ***Elijah the Prophet***.

אֵלִיָּהוּ הַנָּבִיא

PRAYER PRACTICE

Practice reading these siddur words with a partner. Take turns choosing a word for each of you to read.

וְשַׂמְּחֵנוּ	שַׂבְּעֵנוּ	קִדְּשָׁנוּ	וְצִוָּנוּ
וְהִגִּיעָנוּ	וְקִיְּמָנוּ	שֶׁהֶחֱיָנוּ	עָלֵינוּ
מַלְכֵּנוּ	אָבִינוּ	אֲבוֹתֵינוּ	אֱלֹהֵינוּ
עֵינֵינוּ	יִשְׁעֵנוּ	הָיִינוּ	גּוֹאֲלֵנוּ

HEADS UP!

All the words above end in נוּ. נוּ is a suffix that means "us" or "our."

The word אֲנַחְנוּ means "we."

Why do you think so many words in our prayers end with the suffix נוּ?

OUR TRADITION — קִדּוּשׁ

On Friday evening, after we light שַׁבָּת candles, we sing the קִדּוּשׁ over wine. The word קִדּוּשׁ means "making holy." When we sing the קִדּוּשׁ prayer we thank God for making שַׁבָּת a holy day.

The ark where we place the Torah is called the Holy Ark. We call Jerusalem the Holy City, and Israel the Holy Land. Why do you think they are all holy? What or who else do you think is holy?

HOLIDAY QUIZ

Read the name of each holiday. Use the word bank to answer the questions below.

יוֹם כִּפּוּר	פּוּרִים	סֻכּוֹת
שָׁבוּעוֹת	חֲנֻכָּה	

1 We read the מְגִלָּה. What holiday am I? ______

2 We shake the ***lulav*** and eat in a small booth. What holiday am I? ______

3 We celebrate the giving of the Torah. What holiday am I? ______

4 We light the ***hanukkiyah***. What holiday am I? ______

5 We do not eat all day. What holiday am I? ______

מְזוּזָה

LETTERS YOU KNOW. Say the name and sound of each letter.

בּ ת תּ שׁ מ ל כּ ה ר כ ב

ד א ו ק צ ע נ ן ח י ם

ט פּ ס פ ץ שׂ ג

NEW LETTER

ז

VOWELS YOU KNOW. Say the sound of each vowel.

◌ַ ◌ָ ◌ְ ◌ֲ ◌ִ ◌ִי וֹ

◌ֹ ◌ֶ ◌ֱ ◌ֵ ◌ֵי וּ ◌ֻ

ZAYIN

1	זֻ	זוּ	זוֹ	זִ	זְ	זֵי
2	זֶ	שֶׁ	זַ	סַ	זִ	צִ
3	חַז	זָוִי	זַרְ	יִזְ	זֶן	זוֹר

Which Hebrew sound reminds you of a place to see lots of animals?

SHAPE IT UP

What does ***Zayin*** look like?

Close your eyes and picture the letter.

Draw it in the air or use your whole body to make the shape of the letter ***Zayin***.

HEADS UP!

The Hebrew letters ז, ס, צ, and שׂ make similar sounds.

What sound does each letter make?

Read each word carefully.

זְמַן חֶסֶד מִצְוָה שִׂמְחָה

READY, SET, READ

Read aloud all the words that start with a ***Zayin***. Then read all the words that end with a ***Zayin***. Are there words left? Read those too.

1	זֶה	אָז	עֹז	פָּז	בּוּז	זָר
2	זָכֹר	זְמַן	אֹזֶן	חָזָק	חַזָן	אָחַז
3	הַזָן	זֶבַח	זֹאת	מַזָל	זָקֵן	זָהָב
4	יִזְכֹּר	מָעוֹז	זֵכֶר	אֵיזֶה	עֱזֵנוּ	וְזַרְעוֹ
5	זִכָּרוֹן	מִזְבֵּחַ	מַחֲזוֹר	מִזְמוֹר	נֶעֱזָב	זָוִית
6	זְכוּת	מִזְרָח	זְרוֹעַ	מָזוֹן	זַרְעָם	עִזִים
7	זַיִת	הֶחֱזִיר	זָקוּק	הִזְנִיחַ	חֲזַק	וֶאֱמַץ
8	מְזוּזָה	יוֹם	הַזִכָּרוֹן	מַחֲזוֹר	מַזָל	טוֹב

Say מַזָל טוֹב! That means "congratulations"!

I KNOW HEBREW!

Can you find these Hebrew words above?

mezuzah = מְזוּזָה

mahzor = מַחֲזוֹר

Read and circle or highlight them.

PRAYER PRACTICE

Practice reading these siddur phrases. Look for ***Zayin***s as you read. Write the number of words that have a ***Zayin*** on each line.

1	____	הַזָּן אֶת הַכֹּל
2	____	זִכָּרוֹן לְמַעֲשֵׂה בְרֵאשִׁית
3	____	זֵכֶר לִיצִיאַת מִצְרָיִם
4	____	עֵץ חַיִּים הִיא לַמַּחֲזִיקִים בָּהּ
5	____	וְלוֹ הָעֹז וְהַמִּשְׂרָה
6	____	אָז אֶגְמֹר בְּשִׁיר מִזְמוֹר
7	____	וּכְתַבְתָּם עַל מְזֻזוֹת
8	____	עוֹזֵר וּמוֹשִׁיעַ וּמָגֵן
9	____	בַּיָּמִים הָהֵם בַּזְּמַן הַזֶּה
10	____	שֶׁהֶחֱיָנוּ וְקִיְּמָנוּ וְהִגִּיעָנוּ לַזְּמַן הַזֶּה

I SPY

Read aloud the Hebrew words on each line. Circle or highlight the letter in each word that sounds like the English in the box.

1	S	פּוֹרֵשׂ	יִשְׂרָאֵל	שֵׂכֶל	שִׂמְחָה
2	Z	יִזְכֹּר	מַזָּל	זוֹרֵחַ	גְּזֵרָה
3	ACH	מָשִׁיחַ	הִצְלִיחַ	לַמְנַצֵּחַ	מִזְבֵּחַ
4	G	גְּמָרָא	הַגָּדָה	מְגִלָּה	גֶּשֶׁם
5	TS	אֶרֶץ	חָמֵץ	וֶאֱמַץ	קִבּוּץ
6	V	זִיו	זִוּוּג	וְזֹאת	וְזַרְעוֹ

WRITING PRACTICE

ז ל ל

Write the Hebrew word for ***mezuzah***.

מְזוּזָה מְזוּזָה

Write the Hebrew words for ***congratulations***.

מַזָּל טוֹב מַזָּל טוֹב

Write the Hebrew word for ***machzor***.

מַחֲזוֹר מַחֲזוֹר

NAME TAG

Read the name of each letter in the box. Find its matching Hebrew letter and write it on the line. What sound does the letter make?

	Letter name						Answer
1	PAY	כּ	תּ	פּ	ס	בּ	פּ
2	SIN	ל	שׂ	צ	שׁ	ע	
3	GIMMEL	ג	ו	נ	ד	ן	
4	FAY	פּ	כ	ת	בּ	פ	
5	SAMECH	ם	צ	ס	שׂ	ק	
6	TET	מ	ד	ת	ע	ט	
7	YUD	ר	י	ח	ו	נ	
8	HET	ה	ת	ג	ח	כ	
9	NUN	ג	י	ד	ו	נ	
10	ZAYIN	צ	ז	ג	שׂ	ס	

OUR TRADITION — מְזוּזָה

The Hebrew word for "doorpost" is מְזוּזָה. The תּוֹרָה teaches that the שְׁמַע and the וְאָהַבְתָּ prayers should be placed "on the doorposts of your house and on your gates."

That is why we write the words of these prayers on a piece of parchment and place them inside the מְזוּזָה, which is attached to the doorposts of our homes.
מְזוּזָה is the Hebrew word for doorpost

Why do you think the תּוֹרָה teaches us to place the words of the שְׁמַע on the doorposts of our homes?

BE AN ARTIST

Draw a picture to illustrate each Hebrew word or phrase below.
If you want to check what the words mean, look at the מִילוֹן, the dictionary, on page 159.

סִדּוּר

טַלִּית

נֵר תָּמִיד

עֲשֶׂרֶת הַדִּבְּרוֹת

CHECKPOINT CHALLENGE

Play Tic-Tac-Toe with a partner. Take turns reading a word.
If you read a word correctly, mark the square with an X or an O.

שָׁבוּעַ	יִרְבּוּ	גְּאוּלָה
אֵלִיָהוּ	קִדוּשׁ	סְגֻלָה
חֻמָשׁ	מְזוּזָה	צִווּ

כֻּלָם	סִיוּם	טוּבוֹ
תַּלְמוּד	הַלְלוּיָה	בָּרְכוּ
עֻצוּ	סֻכּוֹת	חֲנֻכָּה

צוּר	רְפוּאָה	פּוּרִים
שׁוּבָה	יְרוּשָׁלַיִם	קוּמוּ
זַיִת	מְתֻקָן	שִׁישׁוּ

בָּרוּךְ

Praised, Blessed

NEW LETTER

ךְ

LETTERS YOU KNOW. Say the name and sound of each letter.

בּ ת תּ שׁ מ ל כּ ה ר כ ב

ד א ו ק צ ע נ ן ח י ם

ט פּ ס פ ץ שׂ ג ז

VOWELS YOU KNOW. Say the sound of each vowel.

FINAL CHAF

1 רַךְ כַּךְ בָּךְ לֵךְ לְךָ וּלְךָ

2 אַךְ בְּךָ שֶׁלְךָ בְּכָךְ שִׁמְךָ תֶיךָ

SHAPE IT UP

What does ***Final Chaf*** look like?
Close your eyes and picture the letter.

Draw it in the air or use your whole body to make the shape of the letter ***Final Chaf***.

Make up a clue to remember ***Final Chaf***."

HEADS UP!

Final ךְ is the only final letter that always has a vowel. Read these words.

הַמְבֹרָךְ בֵּיתֶךָ

READING RULE When  comes at the end of a word, the י is silent.

READY, SET, READ

Read aloud each word that ends with a vowel sound ךָ.
Then read aloud each word that ends with ךְ.

1	בָּרוּךְ	אִמֶּךָ	שְׁמֵךְ	עַמְּךָ	דֶּרֶךְ	עָלֶיךָ
2	מֶלֶךְ	לִבְּךָ	רֵעֲךָ	פֶּרֶךְ	אֶרֶךְ	לִבֵּךְ
3	כָּמוֹךָ	צָרִיךְ	הוֹלֵךְ	אֵלֶיךָ	אָבִיךָ	עֻזֶּךָ
4	בָּרוּךְ	בָּנֶיךָ	עִמְּךָ	בֵּיתֶךָ	אוֹתְךָ	כֻּלְּךָ
5	מְבֹרָךְ	יִמְלֹךְ	לְבָבְךָ	יָדֶיךָ	מְאֹדֶךָ	חֻקֶּיךָ
6	לְפָנֶיךָ	עֵינֶיךָ	נַפְשְׁךָ	מְצַוְּךָ	סוֹמֵךְ	מַלְאָךְ
7	בָּרוּךְ	קָדְשָׁתְךָ	בִּשְׁלוֹמֶךָ	אֱלֹהַיִךְ	וַיְבָרֶךְ	
8	תַּנֵּךְ	מִצְווֹתֶיךָ	וּבְלֶכְתְּךָ	וּבְקוּמֶךָ	וּבִשְׁעָרֶיךָ	

I KNOW HEBREW!

Can you find these Hebrew words above?

praised, blessed = בָּרוּךְ

king, ruler = מֶלֶךְ

Read and circle or highlight them.

EXTRA CREDIT

Perhaps you've heard a song about a מֶלֶךְ named דָּוִד.
Can you sing the song and/or do the hand motions that go along with it?

Ask a partner to do it with you!

CLIMB THE LADDERS

Climb up ***Ladder Alef*** by reading words 1-7.
Have your partner climb down ***Ladder Bet*** by reading words 8-14.
Climb up ***Ladder Gimmel*** by reading words 15-21. Have your partner climb down ***Ladder Dalet*** by reading words 22-28. Climbing can be tiring, so make sure to rest in between!

LADDER ד	LADDER ג	LADDER ב	LADDER א
22 אֱלֹהֶיךָ	21 מֶלֶךְ	8 כֶּתֶר	7 כֹּהֵן
23 בָּרוּךְ	20 שֵׂכֶל	9 כֻּלָּם	6 כִּפּוּר
24 לְךָ	19 חֲנֻכָּה	10 כַּוָּנָה	5 כָּבוֹד
25 עַמְּךָ	18 יָכְלוּ	11 עַכְשָׁו	4 כָּשֵׁר
26 דֶּרֶךְ	17 לִכְבוֹד	12 סֻכּוֹת	3 כֹּל
27 לְבָבְךָ	16 בֵּית-כְּנֶסֶת	13 בְּרָכוֹת	2 כּוֹס
28 נַפְשְׁךָ	15 יָכוֹל	14 יִזְכֹּר	1 כַּלָּה

HEADS UP!

There are five letters in the Hebrew alphabet that have a different form when they come at the end of a word.

When a כ comes at the end of a word, it is a final ך.

Can you name three other letters that have a final form?

WRITING PRACTICE

ךְ ך

Write the Hebrew word for ***praised, blessed***.

בָּרוּךְ

Write the Hebrew word for ***king, ruler***.

מֶלֶךְ

RHYME TIME

Read aloud each line. Three words on each line rhyme. Find the word that does not rhyme and write it on the line. Then snap or clap as you read aloud only the rhyming words.

1	דֶּרֶךְ	מֶלֶךְ	שֶׁלְּךָ	אֶרֶךְ	שֶׁלְּךָ
2	קוּמְךָ	בָּרוּךְ	בֵּיתֶךָ	יָדֶךָ	
3	נַפְשְׁךָ	לְבָבְךָ	מְצַוְּךָ	אָרוּךְ	
4	מְאֹדֶךָ	בְּבֵיתֶךָ	מְבֹרָךְ	לְבָבֶךָ	
5	שִׁבְתְּךָ	עָלַיִךְ	דַרְכְּךָ	לֶכְתְּךָ	
6	שְׁלוֹמֵךְ	מַעֲשַׂיִךְ	שְׁעָרֶיךָ	עֵינֶיךָ	

OUR TRADITION — בָּרוּךְ

We have a special way of saying "thank you" to God for God's gifts to us, by saying a בְּרָכָה. The word בָּרוּךְ, which means "blessed" or "praised," is the first word of many blessings.

Below are the six words that begin many of the blessings we recite. Read aloud these words, and then read the concluding phrases that follow.

בָּרוּךְ אַתָּה, יְיָ אֱלֹהֵינוּ, מֶלֶךְ הָעוֹלָם...

Praised are you, Adonai our God, Ruler of the world....

who brings forth bread from the earth.	הַמּוֹצִיא לֶחֶם מִן הָאָרֶץ.	1
who creates the fruit of the vine.	בּוֹרֵא פְּרִי הַגָּפֶן.	2
who creates the fruit of the earth.	בּוֹרֵא פְּרִי הָאֲדָמָה.	3
who creates the fruit of the tree.	בּוֹרֵא פְּרִי הָעֵץ.	4
who creates many kinds of food.	בּוֹרֵא מִינֵי מְזוֹנוֹת.	5
by whose word all things come into being.	שֶׁהַכֹּל נִהְיֶה בִּדְבָרוֹ.	6
for keeping us in life, for sustaining us, and for helping us to reach this day.	שֶׁהֶחֱיָנוּ וְקִיְּמָנוּ וְהִגִּיעָנוּ לַזְּמַן הַזֶּה.	7

SHOW WHAT YOU KNOW

Put a ★ next to the blessing you would say over חַלָּה.

Put a ✔ next to the blessing you would say over wine or grape juice.

List three foods for which would you use the blessing that ends "who creates the fruit of the earth." Draw them here:

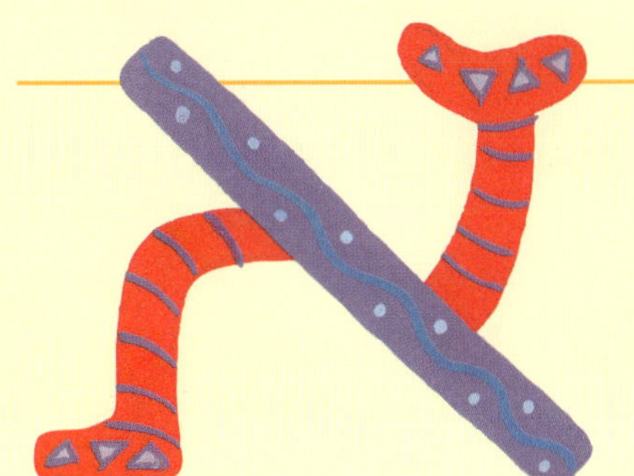

LESSON 25

אָלֶף

Alef

NEW LETTER

ף

LETTERS YOU KNOW. Say the name and sound of each letter.

בּ ת תּ שׁ מ ל כּ ה ר כ ב

ד א ו ק צ ע נ ן ח י ם

ט פּ ס פ ץ שׂ ג ז ך

VOWELS YOU KNOW. Say the sound of each vowel.

1 אַף דַף עוֹף קוֹף גוּף סוֹף

2 כַּף תּוֹף עָף סוֹף תַּף כֵּף

3 יֵף נָף טֶף סָף רַף צוּף

SHAPE IT UP

What does ***Final Fay*** look like?

Close your eyes and picture the letter.

Draw it in the air or use your whole body to make the shape of the letter ***Final Fay***.

Make up a clue to remember ***Final Fay***.

HEADS UP!

When a פ comes at the end of a word, it is a ***Final*** ף.

There are five letters in the Hebrew alphabet that have a different form when they come at the end of a word.

Name the other four letters that have a final form.

READY, SET, READ

The letter ***Final Fay*** makes the sound of the English letter ***F***. Read lines 1-3 to a **f**riend in a **f**unny voice. Read lines 4-6 in a **f**rightened voice. Read lines 7-8 in a **f**ancy voice.

1 נוֹף הֲדַף חַף עָיֵף סַף חוֹף

2 חֹרֶף תֵּיכֶף עֹרֶף עָנָף כֶּסֶף שָׂרַף

3 שֶׁטֶף יוֹסֵף אֶלֶף חָלַף כָּתֵף כָּפַף

4 מוּסָף צָפוּף קְלַף זוֹקֵף קוֹטֵף לָעוּף

5 אָסַף נִשְׂרַף שִׁטּוּף רָצוּף כָּנָף יָחֵף

6 עַפְעַף מְרַחֵף רוֹדֵף שָׁלוֹם זוֹקֵף כְּפוּפִים

7 מְצַפְצֵף לְהִתְאַסֵּף לֶאֱסֹף הֶחֱלִיף לְשַׁפְשֵׁף

8 אָלֶף בֵּית וְצִוָּנוּ לְהִתְעַטֵּף בַּצִיצִית

I KNOW HEBREW!

Can you find these Hebrew words above?

alef = אָלֶף

alef bet = אָלֶף בֵּית

Read and circle or highlight them.

EXTRA CREDIT

Can you find the Hebrew name for Joseph in the lines above? (Hint: The Hebrew name for Joseph begins with the letter ***Yud***.)

Tell a partner what you know about the story of Joseph, the son of יַעֲקֹב and רָחֵל.

Can you find the Hebrew word for peace in the lines above?

Write it in Hebrew here:

____

READING RELAY

In column א, Player 1 reads word 1. Player 2 reads words 1 and 2. Player 3 reads words 1, 2, and 3. Continue the relay until all ten words in the column have been read. Then repeat the Reading Relay with the words in columns ב and ג.

א	
	פּ
1	פָּסוּק
2	פּוֹקֵחַ
3	פֻּרְקָן
4	פְּעָמִים
5	פָּרָשָׁה
6	פּוּרִים
7	פֶּסַח
8	פְּרִי
9	פֶּרֶךְ
10	פָּנִים

ב	
	פּ פ
11	אֲפִיקוֹמָן
12	שׁוֹפָר
13	גֶּפֶן
14	סֵפֶר
15	תְּפִלָּה
16	מַפְטִיר
17	תְּפִלִּין
18	לִפְנֵי
19	מִשְׁפָּחָה
20	תַּפּוּחַ

ג	
	ף
21	כָּנָף
22	אָלֶף
23	קְלַף
24	יוֹסֵף
25	רוֹדֵף
26	מְרַחֵף
27	מוּסָף
28	זוֹקֵף
29	תֵּיכֶף
30	אָסַף

EXTRA CREDIT

Can you find the Hebrew word for ***afikoman***? Write it in Hebrew here:______________

Can you find the Hebrew word for ***Passover***? Write it in Hebrew here:______________

WRITING PRACTICE

ף

Write the Hebrew word for ***alef***.

אָלֶף

Write the Hebrew words for ***alef bet***.

אָלֶף בֵּית

I SPY

Read each line. Circle or highlight the Hebrew letters that sound the same as the English in the box. Write the Hebrew letters on the line.

1	CH	סוֹמֵךְ	לְפָנֶיךָ	תְּפִלִּין	מַלְכוּתְךָ	ך
2	CH	כְּבוֹד	בְּתוֹכֵנוּ	כָּמֹכָה	זוֹכֵר	
3	F	מַפְטִיר	תְּפִלָּה	פָּנִים	אֲפִיקוֹמָן	
4	F	רוֹדֵף	בָּרוּךְ	מוּסָף	זוֹקֵף	
5	M	נוֹפְלִים	כְּפוּפִים	מְפַרְנֵס	הִתְפַּלֵּל	
6	M	מַצּוֹת	מִשְׁפָּטִים	שְׁמוֹ	טוּבוֹ	
7	N	רָצוֹן	אֶרֶץ	הַזָּן	מָזוֹן	
8	N	נֶאֱמָן	נַפְשְׁךָ	מִנְיָן	אָבִי	
9	TS	חָמֵץ	אָמֵן	יַחַץ	עָצִיץ	
10	TS	יִצְחָק	צִיּוֹן	עֶלְיוֹן	צְבָאָם	

HEADS UP!

Five Hebrew letters have final forms. Write the final form of each letter.

נ ____ מ ____ צ ____ כ ____ פ ____

OUR TRADITION — אָלֶף

אָלֶף is the name of the first letter in the Hebrew alphabet. The second letter in the Hebrew alphabet is בֵּית. That is why the name of the Hebrew alphabet is אָלֶף בֵּית.

When we know the letters of the אָלֶף בֵּית, we can read Hebrew words, we can study the Torah, and we can pray from a סִדּוּר.

How does it feel to know that you can read and write all the Hebrew letters and vowels? Write a few of them here.

LETTER NAMES The names of the first ten letters of the אָלֶף בֵּית are in the correct order. The letters at the top are all mixed up. Write the correct letter above its name.

ז בּ	ט ד	ו י	ה א	ח ג
				א
הֵא	דָּלֶת	גִּימֶל	בֵּית	אָלֶף
יוּד	טֵית	חֵית	זַיִן	וָו

ALEF BET CHART

You have learned five new letters in Lessons 20-25.

ף ךְ ז ג שׂ

Turn to the אָלֶף בֵּית chart on page 160. Color in the new letters.

מַזָּל טוֹב! You have learned every letter in the אָלֶף בֵּית. Recite the complete אָלֶף בֵּית.

Give yourself a pat on the back. . . you deserve it!!

SPECIAL RULES

RULE #1

◻ַי ◻ָי ◻ַאי

When ◻ַ , ◻ָ , or א are followed by the letter י at the end of a word, say "EYE" as in "shy" (שַׁי).

1	חַי	אֲזַי	שַׁי	דַי	סִינַי	אוּלַי
2	אֵלַי	מָתַי	שְׂפָתַי	שַׁדַי	הַלְוַאי	בְּוַדַאי
3	אֲדֹנָי	אֱלֹהַי	בְּחַיַי	מִצְווֹתָי	חֻקוֹתַי	רַבּוֹתַי

I KNOW HEBREW!

Find this Hebrew word above.

Live = חַי

Read and circle or highlight it.

HEADS UP!

When וֹ comes after a letter that already has a vowel, it appears like ו וֹ and is pronounced "VOH."

מִצְוֹת = מִצְווֹת

מִצְוֹתָי = מִצְווֹתָי

RULE #2

ךְ

The dot in ךְ tells us it is a ***Final kaf***. There are a few words in the siddur that end with ךָ, pronounced "KAH."

Reading the following siddur words.

אוֹדְךָ	וָאֲחַלְצֶךָ	אֲבָרְכֶךָ	וִיחֻנֶּךָ	יִסְעָדֶךָ

RULE #3

ֶיךָ ָיו

When ֶיךָ or ָיו come at the end of a word, the letter י is silent.

1	דְבָרָיו	אֵלָיו	לְפָנָיו	נִסֶּיךָ	עֵינֶיךָ	חֲסָדֶיךָ
2	עֲבָדֶיךָ	מַעֲשֶׂיךָ	אֱלֹהֶיךָ	לְבָנֶיךָ	וּבִשְׁעָרֶיךָ	
3	מִצְוֹתָיו	רַחֲמָיו	אֱלֹהָיו	בִּמְרוֹמָיו	בְּמִצְוֹתָיו	

Can you find these Hebrew words above? Read and circle or highlight them.

With God's commandments = בְּמִצְוֹתָיו

Your kindnesses = חֲסָדֶיךָ

RULE #4

וֹי וּי

When the vowel וֹ is followed by the letter י at the end of a word, say "OY" as in "boy."

When the vowel וּ is followed by the letter י at the end of a word, say "OOEY" as in "gooey."

1	אוֹי	גוֹי	נוֹי	הוֹי	אֲבוֹי	כּוֹי
2	צִוּוּי	קָנוּי	עָשׂוּי	רָצוּי	גָּלוּי	וִדּוּי
3	פָּנוּי	וַאֲבוֹי	עִלּוּי	בָּנוּי	רָאוּי	שָׁבוּי

RULE #5

יְהֹוָה יְיָ

In the prayer book and in the Torah, God's name is written יְהֹוָה, יְיָ, or אֲדֹנָי.

We pronounce God's name "Adonai" (אֲדֹנָי).

Read the following סִדּוּר phrases. Circle God's name each time you read it.

1 אֲדֹנָי שְׂפָתַי תִּפְתָּח וּפִי יַגִּיד תְּהִלָּתֶךָ

2 בָּרוּךְ אַתָּה יְיָ נוֹתֵן הַתּוֹרָה

3 שְׁמַע יִשְׂרָאֵל יְהֹוָה אֱלֹהֵינוּ יְהֹוָה אֶחָד

4 אַתָּה גִּבּוֹר לְעוֹלָם אֲדֹנָי

5 אַשְׁרֵי הָעָם שֶׁיְיָ אֱלֹהָיו

The סִדּוּר also has many additional names for God. Some of them are underlined below.

Read the following סִדּוּר phrases.

GOD	אֵל אָדוֹן עַל כָּל הַמַּעֲשִׂים	1
GOD	וַיְבָרֶךְ אֱלֹהִים אֶת יוֹם הַשְּׁבִיעִי	2
MY GOD	אֲרוֹמִמְךָ אֱלֹהַי הַמֶּלֶךְ	3
OUR GOD	בָּרוּךְ אַתָּה יְיָ אֱלֹהֵינוּ מֶלֶךְ הָעוֹלָם	4
GOD OF	אֱלֹהֵי אַבְרָהָם, אֱלֹהֵי יִצְחָק, וֵאלֹהֵי יַעֲקֹב	5

RULE #6

כָּל = כֹּל

Sometimes the vowel ָ is pronounced "OH."

1 וּבְכָל נַפְשְׁךָ וּבְכָל מְאֹדֶךָ

2 קֹדֶשׁ קָדְשׁוֹ קָדְשְׁךָ וּבְשָׁכְבְּךָ

3 אָזְנַיִם גָּדְלוֹ עָבְדְּךָ חָפְשִׁי

4 עָזִּי כָּל נִדְרֵי שֶׁבְּכָל הַלֵּילוֹת

RULE #7

ֳ = וֹ

The vowel ֳ is always pronounced "OH."

1 אֳנִיָּה עֳנִי צִפֳּרִים חֳדָשִׁים עֳמָרִים

RULE #8

When the vowel ָ comes before the vowel ֳ in a word, both vowels are pronounced "OH."

1 אָהֳלִים צָהֳרַיִם מָחֳרָת נָעֳמִי צָהֳלָה פָּעֳלִי

שְׁמַע/וְאָהַבְתָּ

שְׁמַע יִשְׂרָאֵל, יְיָ אֱלֹהֵינוּ, יְיָ אֶחָד.
בָּרוּךְ שֵׁם כְּבוֹד מַלְכוּתוֹ לְעוֹלָם וָעֶד.
וְאָהַבְתָּ אֵת יְיָ אֱלֹהֶיךָ
בְּכָל לְבָבְךָ וּבְכָל נַפְשְׁךָ וּבְכָל מְאֹדֶךָ.
וְהָיוּ הַדְּבָרִים הָאֵלֶּה
אֲשֶׁר אָנֹכִי מְצַוְּךָ הַיּוֹם עַל לְבָבֶךָ.
וְשִׁנַּנְתָּם לְבָנֶיךָ וְדִבַּרְתָּ בָּם
בְּשִׁבְתְּךָ בְּבֵיתֶךָ וּבְלֶכְתְּךָ בַדֶּרֶךְ
וּבְשָׁכְבְּךָ וּבְקוּמֶךָ.
וּקְשַׁרְתָּם לְאוֹת עַל יָדֶךָ
וְהָיוּ לְטֹטָפֹת בֵּין עֵינֶיךָ.
וּכְתַבְתָּם עַל מְזֻזוֹת בֵּיתֶךָ וּבִשְׁעָרֶיךָ.

בִּרְכוֹת הַתּוֹרָה

1 בָּרְכוּ אֶת יְיָ הַמְבוֹרָךְ.

2 בָּרוּךְ יְיָ הַמְבוֹרָךְ לְעוֹלָם וָעֶד.

3 בָּרוּךְ אַתָּה יְיָ אֱלֹהֵינוּ מֶלֶךְ הָעוֹלָם,

4 אֲשֶׁר בָּחַר בָּנוּ מִכָּל הָעַמִּים

5 וְנָתַן לָנוּ אֶת תּוֹרָתוֹ.

6 בָּרוּךְ אַתָּה יְיָ נוֹתֵן הַתּוֹרָה.

1 בָּרוּךְ אַתָּה יְיָ אֱלֹהֵינוּ מֶלֶךְ הָעוֹלָם,

2 אֲשֶׁר נָתַן לָנוּ תּוֹרַת אֱמֶת

3 וְחַיֵּי עוֹלָם נָטַע בְּתוֹכֵנוּ.

4 בָּרוּךְ אַתָּה יְיָ נוֹתֵן הַתּוֹרָה.

וְזֹאת הַתּוֹרָה

וְזֹאת הַתּוֹרָה
אֲשֶׁר שָׂם מֹשֶׁה
לִפְנֵי בְּנֵי יִשְׂרָאֵל
עַל פִּי יְיָ בְּיַד מֹשֶׁה.

עֵץ חַיִּים הִיא

עֵץ חַיִּים הִיא לַמַּחֲזִיקִים בָּהּ
וְתֹמְכֶיהָ מְאֻשָּׁר
דְּרָכֶיהָ דַרְכֵי נֹעַם
וְכָל נְתִיבוֹתֶיהָ שָׁלוֹם.

עָלֵינוּ

1 עָלֵינוּ לְשַׁבֵּחַ לַאֲדוֹן הַכֹּל

2 לָתֵת גְּדֻלָּה לְיוֹצֵר בְּרֵאשִׁית.

3 שֶׁלֹּא עָשָׂנוּ כְּגוֹיֵי הָאֲרָצוֹת

4 וְלֹא שָׂמָנוּ כְּמִשְׁפְּחוֹת הָאֲדָמָה...

5 וַאֲנַחְנוּ כּוֹרְעִים וּמִשְׁתַּחֲוִים וּמוֹדִים
לִפְנֵי מֶלֶךְ מַלְכֵי הַמְּלָכִים,

6 הַקָּדוֹשׁ בָּרוּךְ הוּא...

7 וְנֶאֱמַר: וְהָיָה יְיָ לְמֶלֶךְ עַל כָּל הָאָרֶץ

8 בַּיּוֹם הַהוּא יִהְיֶה יְיָ אֶחָד וּשְׁמוֹ אֶחָד.

אֵין כֵּאלֹהֵינוּ

1 אֵין כֵּאלֹהֵינוּ אֵין כַּאדוֹנֵינוּ

2 אֵין כְּמַלְכֵּנוּ אֵין כְּמוֹשִׁיעֵנוּ.

3 מִי כֵאלֹהֵינוּ מִי כַאדוֹנֵינוּ

4 מִי כְמַלְכֵּנוּ מִי כְמוֹשִׁיעֵנוּ.

5 נוֹדֶה לֵאלֹהֵינוּ נוֹדֶה לַאדוֹנֵינוּ

6 נוֹדֶה לְמַלְכֵּנוּ נוֹדֶה לְמוֹשִׁיעֵנוּ.

7 בָּרוּךְ אֱלֹהֵינוּ בָּרוּךְ אֲדוֹנֵינוּ

8 בָּרוּךְ מַלְכֵּנוּ בָּרוּךְ מוֹשִׁיעֵנוּ.

9 אַתָּה הוּא אֱלֹהֵינוּ אַתָּה הוּא אֲדוֹנֵינוּ

10 אַתָּה הוּא מַלְכֵּנוּ אַתָּה הוּא מוֹשִׁיעֵנוּ.

מַה נִשְׁתַּנָּה

מַה נִשְׁתַּנָּה הַלַּיְלָה הַזֶּה מִכָּל הַלֵּילוֹת?

1 שֶׁבְּכָל הַלֵּילוֹת אָנוּ אוֹכְלִין
חָמֵץ וּמַצָּה. הַלַּיְלָה הַזֶּה כֻּלוֹ מַצָּה.

2 שֶׁבְּכָל הַלֵּילוֹת אָנוּ אוֹכְלִין
שְׁאָר יְרָקוֹת. הַלַּיְלָה הַזֶּה מָרוֹר.

3 שֶׁבְּכָל הַלֵּילוֹת אֵין אָנוּ
מַטְבִּילִין אֲפִילוּ פַּעַם אֶחָת. הַלַּיְלָה
הַזֶּה שְׁתֵּי פְעָמִים.

4 שֶׁבְּכָל הַלֵּילוֹת אָנוּ אוֹכְלִין
בֵּין יוֹשְׁבִין וּבֵין מְסֻבִּין.
הַלַּיְלָה הַזֶּה כֻּלָּנוּ מְסֻבִּין.

הַתִּקְוָה

1 כֹּל עוֹד בַּלֵּבָב פְּנִימָה

2 נֶפֶשׁ יְהוּדִי הוֹמִיָּה,

3 וּלְפַאֲתֵי מִזְרָח קָדִימָה,

4 עַיִן לְצִיּוֹן צוֹפִיָּה;

5 עוֹד לֹא אָבְדָה תִּקְוָתֵנוּ,

6 הַתִּקְוָה בַּת שְׁנוֹת אַלְפַּיִם,

7 לִהְיוֹת עַם חָפְשִׁי בְּאַרְצֵנוּ,

8 אֶרֶץ צִיּוֹן וִירוּשָׁלַיִם.

WORD LIST — מִלּוֹן

א	אָדָם	the first human, man
	אַהֲבָה	love
	אֱלֹהִים	God
	אֵלִיָּהוּ הַנָּבִיא	Elijah the prophet
	אָלֶף	*alef*
	אָלֶף בֵּית	*alef bet*
	אָמֵן	amen
	אֱמֶת	truth
	אֲפִיקוֹמָן	*afikoman*
	אֲרוֹן הַקֹּדֶשׁ	the Holy Ark
ב	בְּבַקָּשָׁה	please
	בַּר מִצְוָה	bar mitzvah
	בָּרוּךְ	praised, blessed
	בְּרָכָה	blessing
	בַּת	daughter
	בַּת מִצְוָה	bat mitzvah
ה	הַבְדָּלָה	*havdalah*, separation
	הַגָּדָה	haggadah
	הַמּוֹצִיא	blessing over bread
	הַמּוֹצִיא לֶחֶם	Who brings forth bread
	הַפְטָרָה	Haftarah
	הָרַחֲמָן	the Merciful One (God)
	הַתִּקְוָה	"The Hope", national anthem of Israel
ו	וְאָהַבְתָּ	and you shall love
ח	חַג שָׂמֵחַ	happy holiday
	חַי	live
	חַלָּה	challah, braided bread
	חָמֵץ	leavened food
	חֻמָּשׁ	Five Books of Moses
	חֶסֶד	kindness
ט	טַלִּית	tallit
י	יְהוּדִים	Jews
	יוֹם טוֹב	holiday, festival
	יְצִיאַת מִצְרַיִם	Exodus from Egypt
	יְרוּשָׁלַיִם	Jerusalem
	יָרֵחַ	moon
	יִשְׂרָאֵל	Israel
כ	כַּלָּה	bride
	כִּפָּה	*kippah*, skullcap
ל	לֵב	heart
	לְחַיִּים	to life
מ	מְגִלָּה	scroll
	מָגֵן דָּוִד	Shield of David, Jewish star
	מְזוּזָה	mezuzah
	מַזָּל טוֹב	congratulations
	מַחֲזוֹר	machzor
	מֶלֶךְ	king, ruler
	מַלְכָּה	queen
	מִנְיָן	minyan, ten Jewish adults
	מַצָּה	matzah
	מִצְוָה	commandment
	מִשְׁפָּחָה	family
נ	נָבִיא	prophet
	נֶפֶשׁ	soul
	נֵר תָּמִיד	eternal light
ס	סִדּוּר	prayer book
	סֵדֶר	seder
	סֵפֶר תּוֹרָה	Torah scroll, Five Books of Moses
ע	עִבְרִית	Hebrew
	עֲלִיָּה	*aliyah*, going up
	עֵץ חַיִּים	Tree of Life
	עֲשֶׂרֶת הַדִּבְּרוֹת	Ten Commandments
פ	פֶּסַח	Passover
צ	צְדָקָה	justice
	צִיצִית	fringes on tallit
ק	קַבָּלַת שַׁבָּת	Welcoming Shabbat
	קִדּוּשׁ	Kiddush
	קָדוֹשׁ	holy
	קַדִּישׁ	Kaddish
ר	רֹאשׁ הַשָּׁנָה	Jewish New Year
ש	שַׁבָּת	Shabbat
	שַׁבָּת הַכַּלָּה	the Sabbath Bride
	שַׁבָּת הַמַּלְכָּה	the Sabbath Queen
	שַׁבַּת שָׁלוֹם	a peaceful Shabbat
	שׁוֹפָר	shofar
	שָׁלוֹם	hello, goodbye, peace
	שִׂמְחַת תּוֹרָה	Rejoicing of the Torah
	שְׁמַע	hear
	שַׁמָּשׁ	helper
	שָׁנָה טוֹבָה	Happy New Year
ת	תּוֹרָה	Torah, teaching
	תְּפִלָּה	prayer

אָלֶף בֵּית

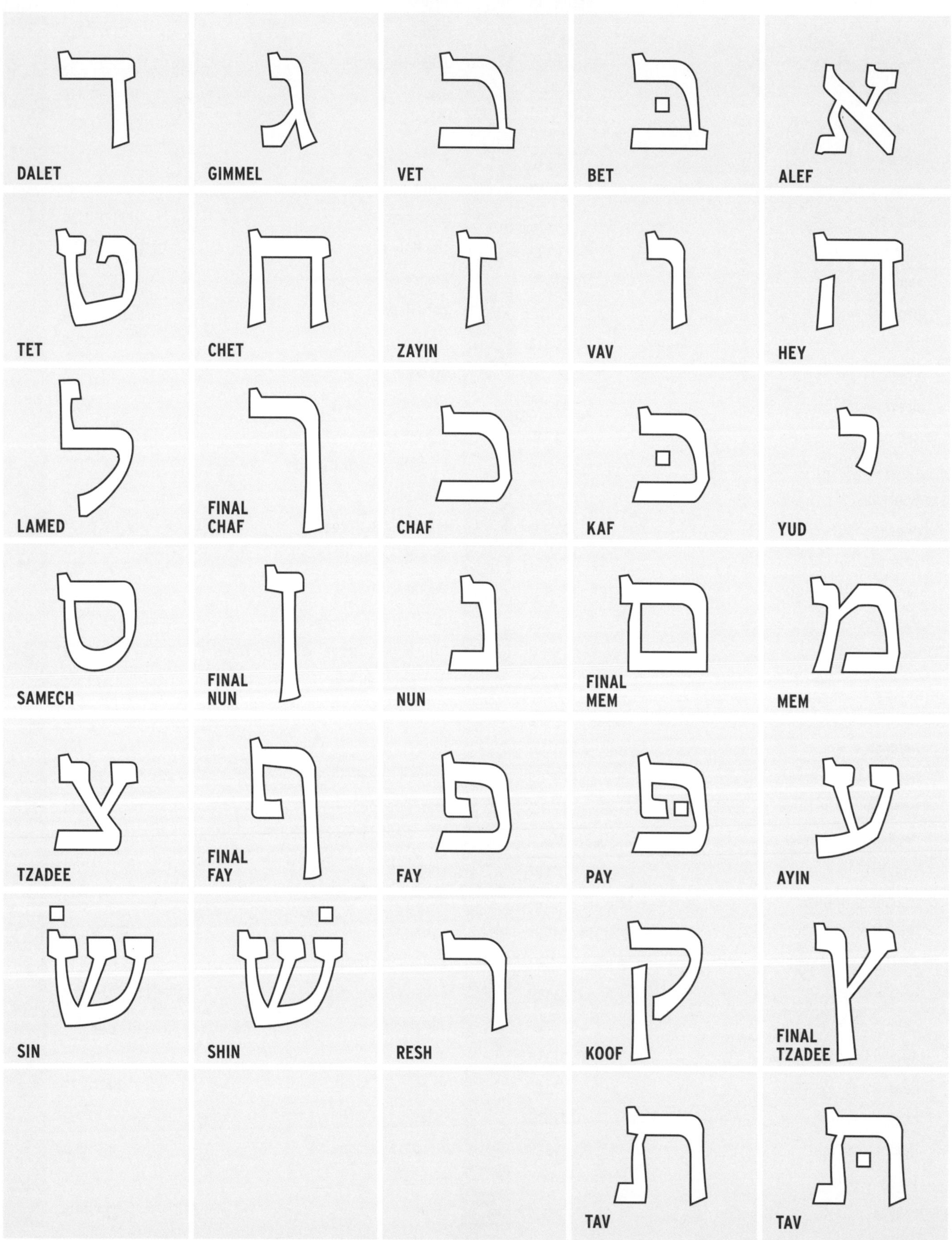

א
ALEF
בּ
BET
ב
VET
ג
GIMMEL
ד
DALET
ה
HEY
ו
VAV
ז
ZAYIN
ח
CHET
ט
TET
י
YUD
כּ
KAF
כ
CHAF
ך
FINAL CHAF
ל
LAMED
מ
MEM
ם
FINAL MEM
נ
NUN
ן
FINAL NUN
ס
SAMECH
ע
AYIN
פּ
PAY
פ
FAY
ף
FINAL FAY
צ
TZADEE
ץ
FINAL TZADEE
ק
KOOF
ר
RESH
שׁ
SHIN
שׂ
SIN
תּ
TAV
ת
TAV